T0312026

Capitalizing Your Technology to Disrupt and Dominate Your Markets

Every business today has some technology as part of its strategy. Inevitably, it is becoming harder for many CEOs to effectively lead their R&D efforts at the same time that their investment in tech keeps growing. Even startup founders can find themselves flustered when trying to understand whether a particular issue is genuinely impossible, getting the team to provide reliable estimates, and having their top tech leaders speak in plain words as opposed to jargon.

This book helps them bridge the culture gap between the C-suite and R&D, covers frequent tech-related decisions and issues, and provides a way to unlock tech as an offensive weapon and a strategic differentiator. To create an environment where technology is not merely an execution mechanism but acts as a fulcrum for strategic opportunities, one must put a particular leadership team in place and equip them with digital literacy.

Based on the author's experience and discussions with hundreds of executives worldwide, he short-circuits common failure patterns and enables nontechnical senior leaders to act with more certainty and clarity regarding their tech efforts. Startups and tech efforts initiated without enough understanding of the technical aspects often have to be scrapped and started from scratch within 18 months. This can make or break certain endeavors, and as the author has helped his clients avoid these problems, the book will help the readers establish a sturdy foundation to work from.

The book covers clear guidelines for founders, executives, and senior leaders that are not tech-savvy. These include establishing a tech organization, making the first key hires, assessing the relevance and risk involved in different options, and creating a healthy connection as opposed to a tech silo. On top of that, it will include lessons and case studies that stem from experience in the "Startup Nation," such as how to inject chutzpah into daily discussions and create an organization with habitual innovation.

Capitalizing Your Technology to Disrupt and Dominate Your Markets

Transforming Cost Centers to Innovation Centers

Aviv Ben-Yosef

CRC Press
Taylor & Francis Group
Boca Raton London New York

CRC Press is an imprint of the
Taylor & Francis Group, an **informa** business
A PRODUCTIVITY PRESS BOOK

First published 2023
by Routledge
605 Third Avenue, New York, NY 10158

and by Routledge
4 Park Square, Milton Park, Abingdon, Oxon, OX14 4RN

Routledge is an imprint of the Taylor & Francis Group, an informa business

ISBN: 9781032415178 (hbk)
ISBN: 9781032415161 (pbk)
ISBN: 9781003358473 (ebk)

DOI: 10.4324/9781003358473

Typeset in Minion
by Deanta Global Publishing Services, Chennai, India

Contents

Acknowledgments

When I was contemplating whether to embark on the adventure to create this book, my biggest and earliest fan supported me wholeheartedly. It just so happens that she is also married to me. My thanks go to Bar, my wife, who is always helpful, insightful, and supportive. Our home, while chaotic at times, also provides great creativity catalysts in the form of three vibrant children: Romy, whose unrelenting positivity I can only hope to mimic; Zoe, with bright and creative thinking that I envy; and Leo, who teaches me daily how fast humans can learn if they put their minds to it.

When I decided at elementary school that I wanted to learn how to program computers, my parents, Naomi and Uri, never hesitated for a second. Since then, no matter what weird requests I made on my quest to learn, they always found a way to make it happen. No child can ask for better support, and I will be forever grateful.

I will be forever indebted to Alan Weiss, my mentor and coach, for my personal growth, for making me envision what is possible, and for forming the best community I have found for like-minded people. Alan, always an exemplar of superb consulting, was indispensable in making this book happen. His community also gave me access to many bright and insightful peers who helped me create this book. Special thanks go to Rebecca Morgan, Hamish MacKenzie, and Adam Bahret for assisting me in writing this book.

Many people helped shape this book, some of whom I do not even know. Thank you to all the beta readers who took their time and provided feedback and to all the executives worldwide who were interviewed and shared their thoughts. Lastly, my greatest appreciation and gratitude go to my clients. No learning happens in a vacuum, and whenever I work with brilliant people, I find that even though I help them, I am often the one learning the most.

About the Author

Aviv Ben-Yosef is an advisor, coach, and consultant for executives and leaders throughout the tech industry. In his consulting business, he has helped companies worldwide, ranging from day-old startups to Fortune 100 companies. By advising, coaching, speaking, and leading strategy workshops, he helps his clients forge teams and cultures they are proud of leading.

Aviv's mission is to help create world-class engineering teams that achieve the unthinkable by upgrading tech from a tool to part of the strategy, amassing Tech Capital, and creating Coders without Borders. In his work as a consultant, Aviv has developed a unique approach to aid software organizations' leadership. Coming from a technical background allows him to "talk shop", yet maintain a business-impact-driven mindset. Aviv's online writing has reached over eight million readers, and his publishing includes multiple blogs, podcasts, videos, and online courses. In 2021, Aviv was inducted into the Million Dollar Consulting® Hall of Fame, which at the time comprised less than one hundred distinguished consultants worldwide.

When not working with clients, Aviv is likely to be spending time with his three children or digging into one of his many hobbies, including reading, collecting and enjoying wine, learning Italian, cooking, traveling, and, of course, coding.

Introduction

For many years, technology hasn't been something one develops in the garage. Today, it should play a center stage role in the strategies and success of many enterprises. Yet one thing hasn't changed during this transition: technology has remained as nebulous and as arcane as a magician's act for most of those not "in the know." Even more concerning, its adoption has been growing across the business landscape like a monster from a Japanese horror film, devouring everything in its path when uncontrolled. Although many senior executives have a better understanding of software and high tech, *that understanding hasn't yet translated into the ability to leverage technology to its fullest potential.*

I have been coding since before I was ten, and around my bar-mitzvah, I was already publishing online columns about cyber security. (I didn't have a lot of hobbies.) Having a front-row seat as a technologist and coder for over two decades during the "start-up nation's" boom taught me something: *it's not the best technology that wins; it's that which is most focused on real-world impact.* During this time, I routinely saw inexperienced 19-year-olds with limited budgets in Israel's Unit 8200 outdo their deep-pocketed, triple-degreed counterparts at the NSA. They weren't smarter, but they were often more zealous and keener to see results. The race does, usually, go to the swift.

Working with hundreds of executives worldwide has taught me the mind-boggling value of this tech-business connection and its rarity. It is almost physically painful for me to watch talented teams waste months going in the wrong direction. Similarly, many CEOs report a fear of missing out on technology and of the "unknown unknowns." Without basic digital literacy, they have to nod along to whatever is being said and can't judge whether it makes sense. Just like I do whenever I take my car to the shop. This digital illiteracy needs to be replaced with "technology as a second language," an observation that also inspired the idea behind this book.

This book was written with these scenarios in mind. If you have an executive role and want to better understand how to exploit the possibilities technology enables, this book is meant for you. You will learn how to communicate better with technological counterparts and how to approach the initiation of tech endeavors. As the unknown unknowns slowly turn to known unknowns, and maybe even known knowns, this should clarify your ability to capitalize on the opportunities technology makes available.

By weaving the tech teams into the fabric of the business, we make those technologists more productive and more motivated. In turn, this results in more effective teams that focus their cognitive prowess on creative solutions as opposed to tech for tech's sake. I hope this will help you create a company with happier, better employees and unlock new and innovative paths to success in your business.

Let's call it "productivity for productivity's sake."

Aviv Ben-Yosef
Hadera, Israel

1

You Don't Need a "Tech Strategy": Why Most Efforts Perform Poorly

Say that you've decided to build your dream house. You bought the perfect lot. A budget is set for the actual construction. You get an architect and a team, show them the lot, and tell them to "get to work." After that, you leave them be for months. The construction team, being professional, tries to do its best. They use fine materials and industry best practices and collaborate to work fast.

A few months pass, and you start wondering what's going on. You pay them a visit only to see that the skeleton isn't even being worked on yet. They are still contemplating different structures and share the "construction strategy" they've been formulating: only certified professionals are hired, a thorough examination process has been put in place, and they are now wrapping up a committee that decided on a color scheme. You gently remind them you'd like to move into this house this year, and they promise to work faster. They simply assumed things needed to be done "properly."

A few more months pass, and you're finally invited to see the house. The construction quality is top-notch, and everything looks good. However, even with a quick glance, you start noticing some issues. For example, a bedroom is missing, and the team says they thought it's ok for two of your kids to share a room, so you get to have an in-house gym. The kitchen is not functional or adjusted to the fact that you're a family that "lives" in the kitchen. And it turns out that a wine cellar was built, at a high cost, even though you don't drink.

Those are just the obvious problems. We haven't even started to talk about the maintenance mismatch. The "construction strategy" assumed you have a green thumb, so the backyard is beautiful but filled with plants and trees that require constant maintenance and care, which you don't have the time for. The high-ceiling windows and skylights look fabulous—but given recent dust storms they will get dirty and require a special cleaning crew a few times a year. The team interpreted your relatively high budget for construction as a willingness to afford high maintenance costs indefinitely. Whoops!

OH, WE WANTED TO TALK ABOUT TECH

I hope this short story didn't scare you too much (I am sure that for some of you, it inevitably triggered some bad memories). As unbelievable as this fib may seem, it accurately (and mind-bogglingly) recounts how many companies are going about their tech efforts: unclear expectations, unverified assumptions, lack of transparency, and virtually no feedback loops. Anywhere you look, you can find packed teams with vast budgets being poured and meager results to show for it.

There are the "digital transformation" stories of companies that have been *transforming* for years with no discernible ROI so far. There are also the failed startups that sunk too much money into projects that didn't generate market interest fast enough. And don't get me started with all the horror stories of CEOs that are now on their third or fourth tech agency, which, *again*, says everything done by their predecessors is subpar and should be rewritten from scratch.

These are just the blatant catastrophes. In fact, most of the efforts aren't as poorly managed but suffer from quickly diminishing returns in any case. They tend to regress for myriad reasons rather than getting better with time. That has become what we expect—you grow and you slow. If you belong to the majority that is not doing abysmally but neither doing great, your tech efforts are probably running like one of these two efforts.

NOTE:

While the principles laid out in this book apply to all leaders in the company, I will address the nontechnical executives and their role in implementing these principles unless otherwise stated.

Scenario A: Short-Leashed Tech

These are the cases where the tech team—in-house, outsourced, or a mix—is not given much agency or autonomy. Instead, it is treated with suspicion and caution. This scenario is often the case in companies where the executive team doesn't have a technical background or has been burned in the past by tech efforts going awry. My conversations with these executives show that this behavior never originates in malice or the wish to micromanage. If you suspect that you are treating your tech team like that, it is likely you have other reasons in mind.

Let us consider some examples. First, there's risk management, especially when it comes to cost. When this isn't your first rodeo, and you've experienced similar endeavors where the budget had to be tripled and deadlines pushed by months or years, who can blame you for keeping your tech team on a short leash? Like our story above, I imagine the second time you'd build a house it would look much different, and we tend to let the pendulum swing too far in the other direction.

Second, lack of trust is often confused with micromanagement. In environments where the engineers fail to provide reliable updates and estimates, it is almost inevitable for leadership to require more frequent updates and scrutinized work plans. That is just the easiest way for most to compensate for lack of clarity and vagueness, which in turn creates mistrust. The members on the team then feel like they are being treated like children and not as the professionals they are.

Teams treated like this are simply incapable of fully utilizing their potential and impact. The stress on short work cycles with low context can successfully keep the budget at bay and create reliable work plans, but at the cost of very tactical output. The team cannot spot opportunities or plan long-term because they are only privy to their current tasks. They become task-completion machines and nothing more.

Scenario B: The Abdication

The other common scenario, which is almost the complete opposite, occurs when the company's leadership gives the tech team carte blanche to do as they please, similar to our construction example earlier. It might not be worded like that. For example, the CEO might believe she's merely following the standard advice of hiring people and getting out of their way. As with everything, the devil is in the details.

When the teams are left on their own, without ongoing feedback and alignment, they are destined to go off-track eventually. In some companies, it is a conscious decision because the other executives don't "understand" technology and therefore shy away from telling *the geeks* what to do. Other times, there might be a genuine product team in place, but it too doesn't collaborate with R&D. Rather than working side-by-side, always in lockstep, silos, processes, and protocols are erected to keep everyone at arm's length.

Even the most competent teams will have a hard time operating in a vacuum. Without continuous contact and communication, things often devolve into an enterprise version of *The Lord of the Flies* where each department focuses on something completely different and entirely disconnected from the company's goals. There is such a thing as too much leeway, and it means that the leadership team is effectively absolving itself of its responsibility to *lead*.

SIDEBAR: WHAT'S "TECH" EXACTLY?

We will cover the importance of bridging the language and jargon gap between business and tech people later, but let us start doing so early. "Technology" is a word that can mean many different things. For high-tech workers, "tech" is used regularly to indicate software in particular. More generally, it could also refer to hardware, such as robotics, sensors, and controllers. In this book, I will use the terms "technology" and "tech" to mainly cover software projects or combined software and hardware products, as these are the types of companies I have worked with extensively.

Spotting the Disconnect

There are a few clear telltale signs that my years of advisory have taught me. Whenever I notice these, I know chances are high that one of the two above scenarios is at play. Consider these and assess how much of your tech organization do they reflect.

> **Complete order-taking mode**: These teams are always busy in execution mode. No one ever bats an eye when asked to do something or questions the idea itself. "Why" is rarely uttered, and therefore the engineers are plowing away without context. They regularly get

things done but don't grok the bigger picture. This often results in frequent do-overs: once a feature is declared as done, someone from the business gives it one look and immediately declares this isn't what they had in mind.

Tech debt focus: We will discuss in more depth later the meaning of jargon commonly tossed around, such as *tech debt* and *refactoring*. For now, suffice it to say that if your R&D department is investing considerable amounts of time into handling its "debt" or has a set chunk of time for doing this (e.g., 20% of every quarter, regardless of other objectives), then it is likely suffering from lack of direction and no focus on impact.

Tech strategies are formed: At first glance, this might seem an innocent part of work. However, my experience shows that these "tech strategies" are more often than not unrelated to the company's actual strategy. They are, in fact, used as a replacement due to the void of real strategy. Either the company has failed to form a clear strategy or to communicate it to the tech organization. Well-run teams shouldn't go off on their own inventing a unique strategy but have endeavors that trace back clearly to some grand vision with clear business goals in mind. No part of the company should have a standalone strategy. There should be one overarching strategy from which other plans derive.

Figure 1.1 shows how these different situations are likely to form due to two factors. First is the team's autonomy. A team without autonomy will usually default to smaller scoped tasks, while a team with it will tend more toward larger-scale endeavors. Second, we have focus as a mechanism for choosing what to do. Without a focus on results, R&D can work a lot but produce little value. This book is about the processes, cultures, and principles the best companies implement to avoid these scenarios.

HOW THIS LIMITS YOUR TEAM TODAY

The modes of operation described above aren't marginally suboptimal. They can make all the difference between an R&D operation that just checks off tasks and one that propels a company to the forefront of its

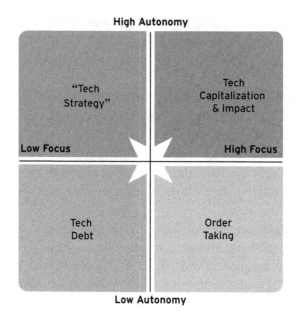

FIGURE 1.1
Influence of autonomy and focus.

industry. The funny thing is that it costs the same to have either, so why settle for the worse one? The difference we're considering here doesn't depend on the team's seniority or talent—these are orthogonal.

The Motivational Pull

What's more, in both modes the team works as hard. It is not the case that in these siloed organizations, you will always find troves of engineers who are counting their days and "dialing it in." You won't see teams sitting doing nothing. Good people try to pour meaning into whatever they do, even when they are not given enough guidance and context.

Lacking any other clear objective, motivated personnel ultimately start down the path of least resistance. They consider where they can feel a sense of accomplishment, growth, impact, and professionalism. For technical people, this often takes on the shape of *tech for tech's sake*. Their motivation pulls them to do something, *anything* really, and they invest in some extra technical gadgetry and cleverness. Once those help them achieve self-actualization—which is the top rung in Maslow's hierarchy of

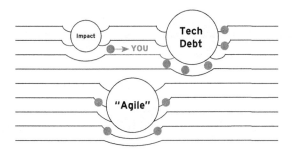

FIGURE 1.2
Motivational pulls.

needs[1]—then they will double down on it. Thus a vicious cycle commences, where R&D is often stuck in a feedback loop which makes them more and more focused on technology and gradually become more disconnected from other parts of the company.

As seen in Figure 1.2, these technical aspects of the work pull them because they are most appealing when there are no other objectives and connections to impact. Pulling the team back to be more impact-oriented requires an extra effort at this point, as anything new you offer will have to provide a pull strong enough to get "escape velocity" from their old habits. Therefore, the sooner you start work on this, the better.

Tragedy of Good Intentions

Given this disconnect and the resulting effects of the motivational pulls, otherwise, great teams routinely miss out on opportunities to capitalize on their talents. First, they frequently act as a form of an internal software factory, meaning they churn out work—sometimes quickly—but provide little insights and engagement. These software factories might feel cooperative initially. You ask for something, and they immediately run off to start working on it. This is precisely what we don't want to see, though. Healthy partnerships and collaboration mindsets would result in discussions about possibilities to do things differently than initially asked so that the team could save on costs, time or even provide more value to its customers.

Second, when these teams are disconnected from the rest of the business, they usually fail to see what's coming ahead. That is how we routinely see companies that have a booming business but then stop in their tracks when the tech team cannot keep up. Some examples I routinely see include teams that were "surprised" by the need to support clients on other continents whereby the existing tech infrastructure wasn't built to support that, or where a particular business model change or evolution is rendered unfeasible because the team never considered it before and would take too long to be made operational. Engineering departments attuned to the company's direction and strategy can often sense what's coming ahead and start taking small steps to enable these changes should they become a reality.

Lastly, this focus on technology also means that your brightest people are not spending their brain cycles thinking about innovation that could help move the business forward. Their creativity will revolve mainly around creating sophisticated tech tools and tech fads, thus losing out on a major part of the knowledge worker—their ability to bring in novelty and improvements.

STOP TELLING YOURSELF THESE

Before we go on to cover how the best teams do this differently, we have to address your mindset. You will never be able to transform your tech to a high-efficacy one if you keep telling yourself the below excuses. This thinking isn't uncommon. In fact, I regularly hear all of these excuses. Since I cannot hear from you which of these are holding you back, I will list the most typical ones and refute them. Refer back to this as you're reading if you hear a nagging voice in the back of your head trying to make this case again.

I Don't Know How to Manage R&D

Frequently used as a reason to act very hands-off with the tech team is to admit you don't know how they should operate and run off. Some even take it a step further and claim that they don't understand "all this tech stuff" and therefore have no input to the matter anyway. This couldn't be farther from the truth.

There is no real need for you to be an expert in a field, as a CEO or senior executive, to provide your guidance there. I've worked with many chief executives, and I guarantee that not a single one was an expert in all of R&D, Product, Sales, Marketing, Customer Success, and the many other things required to operate an enterprise successfully. Why is technology the one area where we are quick to cut ourselves too much slack and disengage?

With most other areas of a company, the CEOs feel comfortable with appointing an executive or manager to run them while "keeping their finger on the pulse." Technology is no different.

They Should Know How to Manage Themselves

Perhaps another side of the coin for the last excuse is when you explain to yourself that these highly paid experts should be capable of doing things by themselves—and shouldn't require your time and focus. Again, this doesn't hold up with any other department and cannot be the case with technology. Yes, experienced professionals should be able to make many decisions independently and not require constant handholding.

Nevertheless, every single part of your company has to get ongoing directions and feedback to ensure that things are going on the right path. Otherwise, they will eventually drift apart from the rest of the business, as described above.

We're Too Busy to Take Care of Them

I once worked with a CEO who declared he had too many things to do and therefore talked with his CTO for about five minutes every couple of months unless something went wrong. This being a unicorn startup that relied on technology for its success didn't help. Despite the fact that the CTO was highly motivated, business-oriented, and capable, it was inevitable for a gap to form with such a lack of communication.

The company missed out on many possible innovations that the R&D team could have produced—some of which were requested by others in the company many months after the tech team had already suggested them. The CEO failed to understand the work performed by the tech team and how it was subjectively superior to groups of similar budgets and circumstances. That ultimately resulted in whole quarters of suboptimal work and back-and-forth that could have been avoided with an embarrassingly simple fix: communication.

If you cannot afford to talk to all your executives and senior leaders regularly, you probably should be talking to them even more until the situation is improved. Letting departments sit in solitude is never the solution for busyness, just a recipe for more of it.

They Want the Autonomy

The last typical excuse is that the team is actually happy to be left alone. Some leaders even feel like they're supposed to disengage from teams and that giving them direction is "micromanagement." Common startup lore has created this impression. Consider the famous Steve Jobs quote, "It doesn't make sense to hire smart people and then tell them what to do. We hire smart people so they can tell us what to do."[2] Taking such advice at face value is a terrible idea. If you know anything about Steve Jobs, you know he did his fair share of telling people what to do.

The magic lies in the altitude of the discussion. Clearly, there's no sense in telling your engineers how to write code or second-guessing the precise location of buttons on your website that the user-experience team put thought and research into. These directions are too low-level and encroach on your people's areas of expertise. When teams ask for more autonomy, these are the problems they often have in mind. They do not want to be told what to do at that level.

Nevertheless, do not assume this is the only possible option for providing guidance. Telling the team which needs are most important to the company at the moment and providing high-level business objectives can be priceless in capitalizing on tech efforts. Confiding with them about the genuine obstacles the company might be facing, its current appetite for risk, and similar context can open the floodgates for innovation and creativity.

The best executives and teams I work with are vying for this sort of input and guidance. After all, we all want our work to mean something, and knowing what your target is makes that possibility tangible. Whenever communicating with your tech leaders, keep Figure 1.3 in mind. You shouldn't be so disengaged that you're above the clouds and cannot see what they are doing, but you also shouldn't be deep in the weeds that you

FIGURE 1.3
Altitude of engagement.

are intruding on the team's freedom. Like Goldilocks, you have to find the altitude that's "just right." This often also solves the lack of time described in the previous excuse.

WHAT THE BEST LOOKS LIKE

Assuming you are now more aware of some of the mistakes you've been making, the rest of the book will help you put these principles into practice. To help you grok what you should be aiming for and what is possible, we will first cover some of the repeating attributes I have seen with the best teams I've worked with worldwide.

Breaking Silos

The first concept is to eliminate the notion that R&D should be isolated from the rest of the company or protected from any interaction with the "real world." Just because the engineers' time is costly doesn't mean we should aim to have them streamlined like a manufacturing production line.

Silos come in all shapes and sizes. Spotify is known[3] for breaking silos even within its engineering departments. They established cross-functional teams where all different disciplines related to product engineering worked together in a single "squad." Thus they removed communication and bureaucracy barriers and created teams capable of delivering business objectives end-to-end.

This also applies outside of pure engineering roles. For example, many companies are now making collaboration the default by having these squads include product managers, UX designers, data scientists, analysts, and sometimes even the relevant marketing and sales personnel. This is the complete opposite of the dreaded IT department that must only be communicated with through pedantically formatted tickets.

Imagine trying to get your house built and none of the different professionals were talking to each other. The gorgeous marble countertop arrives, and you find out it doesn't match the plan for the electric wiring needed. Things will have to be fixed or completely redone at extra cost and time. This failure work could have been avoided.

Fusing Engineers with the Business

A similar practice ensures that engineers are made aware of the "outside world." They should regularly see the effects of their work on the customers and the company's bottom line. They should hear feedback, both positive and negative.

One company founder told me how, due to a demand overload, everyone in the company had to take shifts answering customer requests and helping the customer success team. He recounted how after the engineers got to see in their own eyes how the customers were interacting with the product and getting frustrated, the teams were able to later come up with improvements that no one had considered before. That was enough for the company to turn this emergency operation mode into an ongoing tradition: everyone shadowed customer success from time to time.

Similarly, the fusing should include making the team work at a higher altitude. Providing your tech team with high-level goals and letting them try and solve them as opposed to keeping them on a short leash and only giving them tasks is essential. It both connects them to the actual business and helps them work more effectively.

CASE STUDY: THE IMPACT ORIENTATION

I was brought in to help a startup that seemed to be working too slowly. They had a brilliant and experienced team, and everyone was highly motivated. However, communication was abysmal, work wasn't prioritized correctly, and there was significant politics even though the company was relatively young.

Mapping the different issues with the leadership team, it was clear to me that their attempts to work in silos, along with the short leash and limited scope, were preventing them from fulfilling their potential. We instituted cross-functional teams, fused them with the Product and Marketing professionals as needed, and created business-level, empowering objectives for the teams to work on, as opposed to being handed small, too well-defined tasks.

Within two months, clear progress was already visible. The company published its most significant product improvement in years. During a retrospective, one of the VPs said, "We did this 3-4 times faster than we used to work." No one was staying long hours to type three times more every day! They had learned how to capitalize on their existing tech talent.

Tech as a Strategy, Not a Tech Strategy

I hope that by this point, it is clear that a separate "tech strategy" that the engineering team works on by itself is a bad idea. However, that doesn't justify a strategy that doesn't take technology into consideration. While this might seem straightforward, I regularly come across companies that consider themselves "high-tech startups" but do not rely on technology in any substantial way as part of their plan.

For example, I once talked to a couple of cofounders working on a venture that essentially copied a simple existing product but relied on their regulatory lobbying to generate business in a specific locality. While they did *depend* on technology for part of their vision, it certainly wasn't part of their strategy. It was merely a tool. Because they were planning on getting captive customers, they didn't care about user experience, great value, or any innovation. Now, this is a legitimate business, but certainly not one that should be classified as a tech startup. Their problem was that they didn't realize this gap and therefore had ended up creating a tech team that wasn't the right one for their needs. For their specific scenario, they should have gotten a team that is experienced with working in highly regulated areas and less focused on user experience, at least for the first few versions. They had the exact opposite, resulting in endless back-and-forth cycles with the regulator.

Contrast that with companies where technology is one of the tenets of the strategy. As someone who facilitates Sentient Strategy®⁴ sessions, I'm used to talking to executives about their company's 2–3 *strategic factors*. It's OK to have factors such as market, patents, or methods of sale and distribution. However, if technology isn't one of your strategic factors, you will not likely fulfill its potential. Going back to our analogy, picture how more effective things will be when those constructing your house would share your vision of what "home" means for your family and how your ideal days will look like.

Making Time for Innovation

One last core principle is that we commit to viewing R&D as an innovation center, not a cost center. Relating to the previous point, many companies view their tech efforts solely as a cost. That attitude affects all levels of the R&D group, especially how your key tech leaders are likely to consider their role. When a good manager is in charge of a cost center, she focuses on lowering costs and productivity. While those aspects shouldn't be neglected, they don't represent the epitome of a successful tech operation.

You might be used to the opposite of a cost center being a profit center, and you'd be right, at least partially. That's one option, and in some cases, the tech group can trace its output directly to more profits. One example would be companies that sell algorithms and unique IP, such as OpenAI and DeepMind. However, that's often not that straightforward. Nevertheless, we shouldn't give up on viewing R&D as a value generator.

For that, I teach companies to aim to have their tech department be an *innovation center*. That means that the team is still charged with delivering capabilities in a sustainable, economical, and predictable manner but also makes it part of its role to be creative. Innovation and novelty rarely manifest, though, when the team is constantly working at 100% capacity. No great invention happens when every engineer is strapped for time.

When we are stressed, we stick to our comfort zones. We do what's safe, not what's special. That is perfectly fine for the majority of the work, but not when it becomes the only way of doing the work. And no, having a day or two of hackathons once a year is not enough.

Making innovation habitual, by making time for it and cultivating a culture that expects it, can make your team generate value indefinitely. I've helped companies embrace these concepts. Those, in turn, saw new products emerge, entirely new business models, faster deals closing, better salesforce utilization, improved efficacy throughout the company, and an increase in morale and engagement. You can also remain in the software feature factory mindset and forget about this. I don't think that's much of a choice.

SUMMARY

We've seen how leaving technology teams to their own devices without a healthy and constant stream of communication between them and the business always results in suboptimal performance—at best. The limitations of such models were discussed, along with the usual suspects for why we get ourselves into such situations in the first place.

The most important part is the end, where you saw axioms of great tech utilization and examples of how those benefit real-world companies. While some or all of those rules might seem foreign at this point, we will translate those into actionable steps to help ensure that your team doesn't become another failure story.

Action Items

To ensure that this doesn't remain a theoretical exercise for you, dear reader, I will suggest steps for you to take right now before moving on to the next chapter.

- Consider the continuum between the two scenarios described earlier. Where would you place your company currently between keeping tech on a short leash and completely abdicating? Why?
- Which of the limitations are most evident in your current mode of operation?

- Reading the excuses, which ones do you tell yourself? Which represent the viewpoints of your senior executives?
- Review the excuses, the best practices, and the successful examples with your tech leadership. Which parts resonate the most? Those are likely those that you should start addressing first. Quick wins are how we start building momentum.

NOTES

1. https://en.wikipedia.org/wiki/Maslow's_hierarchy_of_needs.
2. Steve Jobs, *Steve Jobs: His Own Words and Wisdom*, Cupertino Silicon Valley Press, 2011.
3. See Henrik Kniberg's original article from 2012. https://blog.crisp.se/2012/11/14/henrikkniberg/scaling-agile-at-spotify.
4. A methodology introduced by Alan Weiss. https://alanweiss.com/growth-experiences/sentient-strategy/.

2

Geeks in the Boardroom: Tech Leaders Should Take the Lead

A first step in positioning technology correctly is to make sure it has a seat at the table. Technology can only be brought to its fullest potential by treating it as a first-class citizen. With a clear strategic vision, tech executives can best ensure their organizations are ready for what is coming down the road. Even more so, if they speak up, they can help improve upon the strategy in a way that best leverages their team. Creating a healthy structure and division of responsibility is sometimes unclear to nontechnical executives, and the titles don't always make sense. This chapter will cover these topics and help you assess how best to staff your executive team.

THE ROLE OF TECH EXECUTIVES IN YOUR COMPANY

Many nontechnical executives believe that software represents mere tools for execution and doesn't merit strategic input status. However, my experience demonstrates that technology is a prerequisite for an effective corporate strategy.

Having worked with many business founders who started off without a technical partner, I have seen the same story repeat itself. Either because the founders didn't find it necessary or because they couldn't easily find a technological counterpart, they decided to set up shop without one and make do. Some hire an engineering manager to be in charge of the tech effort. Others, often the more product-inclined, might try and direct the

DOI: 10.4324/9781003358473-2

tech people themselves during the first years. Virtually all of them change their minds on these setups a year or two down the line and say that they would have done things differently had they known. A technical partner or genuine executive can be priceless.

Going It Alone

First, I'll make a case for a technical partner for those of you still in the embryonic stages of your enterprise. I worked with a CEO of a new startup with an incredible track record. Having easily secured funding from reputable investors, the company was off to a good start with a hired CTO who took charge of the technical team. When, a few months later, things between the two didn't go well, the CEO regretted the situation:

> No one told me the sheer importance of the tech part and how alone and isolated it would be to lead an organization without a genuine partner that understands this world. I feel alone, and every decision I make feels like it can be a terrible mistake.

The company suffered setbacks in its first years, with a few tech leaders leaving or being replaced, which hurt morale and momentum. It is not easy to staff a CTO position for the third time, and many high-caliber hires will be suspicious when approached about such an opening. While I can attest that with some help, they are now doing splendidly, there's no denying that this suboptimal start cost the company time and money (and who knows how many sleepless nights for the CEO). Having seen the same story play out time after time, I believe it is better to have a technical partner in new enterprises than attempt to hire one later.

Short-Term Benefits

Before discussing the long-term advantages of tech executives, I'd like to start with the more obvious areas. These are the tactical areas where many decisions are needed with immediate effect. As humans—and especially as overwhelmed leaders—we tend to put off anything that is not urgent.

Software engineering requires a mind-boggling number of decisions to be made regularly. The term "engineering" is misleading to many, as in the vast majority of cases, there are no objective measures that can be used to measure the productivity of a team and their solutions. Therefore, an experienced leader can dramatically alter the way resources and time are invested and staff teams in entirely different schemes. That is because experience brings with it a set of intuitions and the ability to detect certain patterns faster than would otherwise be possible.

CEOs I talked to who didn't have a tech executive but used a low-level manager or outsourced services estimated that the effect amounted to a 20–50% difference in R&D budget and at least doubled their time to market. That is because they lacked someone with a drive to optimize decisions and the agency to guide the efforts in the right direction. Technology requires many trade-offs. After all, the fact that almost anything is possible means that there are too many possibilities to choose from. The right leader can help make such decisions faster and in a way that is more attuned to the business's needs.

Understandably, many of these decisions are more tactical and might seem as if they don't warrant an executive. The following sections should make that part of the role definition clearer.

Long-Term Advantages

In a recent poll, nearly 60% of non-IT employees described their company's tech executive as a "strategic advisor who proactively identifies business opportunities and makes recommendations."[1] The fact that this is already the perceived state for most workers should make it clear that tech executives have a great deal of value to provide for your company's strategy.

Consider the rapid rate at which technology is evolving. Improvements are happening so fast that talented software engineers are finding it hard to keep up. What chance does a team of incredibly busy nontechnical executives stand? You need someone on your side to constantly think about the role of technology in your company's future and keep an eye out for what lies ahead. For example, that means they can spot opportunities where it makes sense to embark on research activities and the development of proofs of concept. Anything short of that, and you're destined to be missing too many significant shifts and opportunities that your competitors might be better attuned to.

It is easy to underestimate the impact of such advances, but these greatly compound with time. At its most superficial level, tech executives in your boardroom can first be better apprised of whatever is coming their way, ensuring that their organizations are prepared for these developments. An unfortunately frequent occurrence in many companies is that the CTO is approached with a certain need and can only think, "Had they told me about this three months ago when it was initially considered, we would have been better suited to address this need." Without this fundamental transparency, your senior leaders won't genuinely lead but merely follow orders.

This applies to any sort of initiative, ranging from simple features, through compliance efforts, to strategic endeavors. Merely knowing what is coming up and being prepared for it can considerably increase the R&D team's efficacy.

Moreover, done correctly, their presence should generate an active influence on the company's strategy and direction. Any executive should be engaged in the boardroom and not merely a spectator. Applied to tech, it means uncovering areas where tech can disrupt the "way things are" or shed light on capabilities that might seem impossible to others.

The tech-savvy and those equipped with an inquisitive and product-directed mindset can often spot creative approaches for acting differently. When I hear others say, "That's just not the way it is done," I know that the tech executives are doing their job of challenging the status quo. Without doing so, nothing novel would ever take place.

THE IMPLODING ACQUISITION

A European-based startup was doing well, with its business growing. However, the company's CTO was not treated as a genuine executive, but mostly as a manager with a vanity title. He was not privy to strategic discussions. The founders simply did not comprehend why that mattered. One day, he was told, along with the rest of the leadership team, that the company has signed an agreement to acquire a smaller startup *for its technology*. That was the first time he had heard about the deal and that company!

You can guess what happens next. In the following weeks, he and his senior staff started assessing the acquired company to come up with a plan about integrating the technology and the engineers. It quickly became clear that the technology stacks between the two companies were substantially different, and that any integration would require months of work and perhaps significant rewrites to the acquired solution. When the engineers at the acquired company realized how much uncertainty there was, virtually all of them left.

The acquiring company was left without usable technology, without the talented team members, and without the price it had paid. Several months later, the team was still scrambling to try and salvage something from the acquisition. I can only assume that was the last time the CTO was not invited to strategy sessions. While this is an extreme example, many companies suffer from similar problematic patterns that, with time, cost them a fortune.

Talent Maximization

Another area that might seem minor, but which can significantly influence the efficacy of an R&D team, is how good its talent is. The tech-sector employee market is currently hypercompetitive, and the competition is tougher than ever. The "remote revolution" means that your company is, theoretically, in a match with any other company in the world.

A considerable part of deciding where to work, especially for challenge and personal-growth seekers, is who will be one's manager and the entire leadership team. Savvy engineers already know to look up and ensure that R&D is treated as a first-class citizen in the company, including the standing of its tech leadership. They would not be wrong to assume that an insubstantial sway for tech in the boardroom is likely to be less challenging, fulfilling, and innovative.

WITH GREAT RESPONSIBILITY SHOULD COME GREAT POWER

Some of you might remember a famous quote from Spiderman: "With great power comes great responsibility." There is no denying that the leaders in charge of tech efforts have an enormous responsibility that can sometimes make or break a business. Most tech organizations involve a formidable R&D budget which, on average, amounts to 10–30% of revenue. The headcount can be so great that it has a significant "pull" that shapes the company's culture. The leaders of these teams can completely derail strategic efforts or enable market disruption and innovation.

Because of this, it is imprudent to view these leaders as accountable and responsible and not accept their power. Like it or not, they influence the company's momentum significantly, which is reason enough to stop treating them as mere managers. When given the power, they will be able to wield that power for good. However, when they are withheld enough autonomy and are not viewed as peers by the rest of the executive team, their lack of visibility into the rest of the business will harm the company.

Avoiding Glorified Managers

First, I want to speak against the common practice of handing out empty vanity titles. I've worked with countless "VPs of …" or "Heads of …" that were not genuine executives. It is sometimes also the case with C-level executives or even cofounders. While their title might literally mean that they are executives in the company, they were not regarded as such by their peers or the CEO.

These leaders holding shiny titles void of meaning are what I refer to as *Glorified Managers*. Their scope of influence is limited in awkward ways. Frequently, they can rack up six-figure cloud bills with no one batting an eye, yet need to get approval to bring in an external expert, promote a manager, or even expense $50 for an online course. Incredibly enough, this dissonance is something many are blind to until it is expressly pointed out.

One major problem with glorified managers is that they lack agency. That manifests in a lack of ability to seize opportunities such as those long-term effects described above. Further, other executives don't view them as their peers, yet hold them accountable for execution. Accountability without authority creates learned helplessness in tech organizations that eventually learn to treat any request as a last-ditch effort. I believe this plays a significant role in the formation of the "IT as adversary" stereotype (or, perhaps more correct, archetype).

These glorified managers are often not privy to strategic discussions and are not invited to partake in board meetings or forums where roadmaps are formed. Therefore, they cannot move "upstream" to leverage their capabilities to their full potential. Moving upstream refers to leaders going up from the level of order-taking managers who merely receive orders and execute, all the way to where these decisions are coming from. Only at that altitude can they understand the "why" behind requests to perform them correctly or change the company's course to reach other decisions in the first place. If you've already created these glorified managers in your organization, I recommend having a new expectation-setting conversation and essentially telling them things are restarting with a blank slate. It is rare that people make a transition so radical after getting used to a certain level of engagement without *very* clear language and witnessing the CEO's commitment to it.

The case for tech executives, though, doesn't end here.

The Hard Decisions

Fully capitalizing on technology's promise often requires executive teams to make tough calls that require political influence in the company. As with many strategic endeavors, it is easy to trade off the potential long-term gains to maintain the status quo and enjoy its short-term comfort and security. However, we know that no market disruption or innovative leaps are achieved by teams that are hunkered down and ensconced within their comfort zones.

Exploiting a technological opportunity might not be possible without an executive championing it. By "selling" the advantages to other stakeholders, gaining alliances throughout the company, and applying gravitas and sway within the organization, they can help push for fearless advancements. Such feats are not likely to be achieved by a glorified manager.

CASE STUDY: SOFTWARE-AS-A-SERVICE OR BUST

A promising startup I was advising was approaching product-market fit. Their pipeline was incredible. The reviews were terrific. The founders were satisfied and plowing full speed ahead. The crux of the issue was that this business-to-enterprise solution was unsustainable.

The contracts and the salespeople's promises stacked piles of busy-work on the tech team. The product was intended to be a Software-as-a-Service (SaaS) offering. However, they were still welcoming on-premise setups, something which was only meant to be done for the first handful of design partners. Those opting for the cloud solution, though, were given life-cycle promises that would cripple enterprises, let alone a budding startup.

The VP of Engineering saw this was not tenable and that at the current pace, his team would have to double in size to keep fixing bugs. That was without any new features! Unfortunately, he did not have enough sway, and the company continued to sign contracts it ended up regretting. No salesperson wanted to harm their closing rates because that glorified manager said it was a problem.

Eventually, with a lot of persuasion from myself and another global expert, the CEO harkened, and the company changed its strategy. It was only because we spoke about business needs and not about engineering overhead or technical debt. The team increased velocity, and the company became a category leader that leveraged the opportunities the COVID pandemic had offered. The VP, however, stepped aside. Only then did the CEO acknowledge the need for a genuine tech executive.

Some technological advancements are only enabled by getting others in the company to change their ways or by changing the company's business model entirely. Such changes are never easy to initiate, even for founding CEOs. Therefore, a strong, experienced, and highly regarded technological presence in the C-suite is a prerequisite to embarking on such changes. These tech executives, who speak both technology and business, can bridge the gap between the two worlds and help achieve what would otherwise be impossible.

Similarly, we need leaders who have an understanding of the business and the acumen of communicating it so they will be listened to. I saw a company with two brilliant nontechnical founders completely disregarding the suggestions of their CTO about a request they'd made. They simply didn't view the CTO's opinion as worthwhile—given his tendency to focus on shiny objects and technological buzzwords. This can be immediately traced to the company wasting more than a quarter at a time when they were running out of runway. This wasted effort and time could have been avoided in a ten-minute discussion with a genuine tech executive (that is quite literally the time it took me to make them realize the mistake).

Any strategy worth pursuing will need a champion for its tech angle, be it for inward-looking changes (such as new systems or ways of doing the work in the company) or for external adaptations (e.g., like the new business model and offering as covered in the case study above). These hard decisions should be a major part of the responsibility of your tech leaders.

R&D Gatekeepers

A final angle for boardroom geeks is that R&D has a de facto veto on much of the business. For example, many ideas can be shot down immediately by stating they are infeasible or providing level-of-effort estimates that require too much time or money. These objections are not necessarily malicious but naturally occur as part of the adversarial relationship described earlier. The company, therefore, benefits from treating R&D as a partner to other stakeholders instead of an adversary.

Similarly, tech leaders cannot allow themselves to be glorified managers. They need to be strategic partners to instill purpose in their people and achieve buy-in for the different efforts. Creating such a partnership with the rest of the company flips the "possibility switch" on: rather than dismiss things right out of the gate, the eager team will apply a suspension of disbelief for long enough to come up with a solution or, at the least, with close enough alternatives.

R&D organizations can make or break most plans, dealing them death by a thousand paper cuts. Presented with an initiative they do not understand or are opposed to, they can easily point out many possible issues, require extra time or staff due to different "technological debt" or "refactorings" that are needed, and so on. While this is endemic in corporations and companies that do not view their tech operations as strategic, I hardly ever come across it when dealing with companies that have made the decision to treat the tech team as an equal partner.

RESPONSIBILITIES OF TECH EXECUTIVES

Hopefully, you should now be inclined to bring in a technological leader to your executive team. The next step is to define the role of this tech executive, so you can maximize your chances of staffing the position successfully. A good hire will act as a force multiplier for the company, while a bad one can turn out as a glorified manager or worse. To help you define this role correctly, let us go over tech executives' common responsibilities and archetypes.

To make these more approachable, the responsibilities will first be described from the viewpoint of the problems they are meant to solve. After covering these problem areas, you will see how these map to the different tech executive archetypes.

What Is Your Technological Edge?

The first question is often about the technology itself. Given all the different options available, which technologies should you start working on and which should you start researching? What sort of innovation do you need to create in-house, and which capabilities can be brought in quickly? How do you create a solution that is feasible, can scale with the business's needs, and is viable given its costs and risks?

Think about the difference between a website a high-schooler creates for you during their summer break as opposed to the scalable, reliable, and secure solution that a professional tech team would produce. The former might be running haphazardly on someone's single server somewhere, prone to power outages and novice hackers. The latter is likely to be installed on one of the major cloud providers, using best-of-breed tools that provide commensurate results and peace of mind.

How Do You Create This Technology?

Having a clear vision of which technological solutions make sense is only part of the puzzle. The more challenging part is translating these plans for technology into working solutions. Professionals often call the plan the "architecture," and turning that into real software is called "implementation" or "delivery." The delivery will require more personnel than coming up with the architecture, similar to an actual building's architecture done by a handful of architects but then constructed by many workers.

Being in charge of the implementation work includes managing the different engineers and other professionals, communicating with stakeholders, hiring and staffing the team, etc. This person need not be the brightest techie in your organization but should be experienced in the work to bridge the tech people and the rest of the company.

What Problems Should Technology Solve for Your Customers?

Customers can rarely envision what is possible. Developing effective solutions for them requires *product leadership*. A senior product manager will help shape the product vision and perform product discovery to flesh out the most dramatic developments.

Strictly speaking, product management does not necessarily require a technological background. Nevertheless, product and R&D are joined at the hip—one cannot succeed without the other. Therefore, I highly recommend viewing this as one big block: product engineering. Often, there are two different executives in charge of the product leadership and R&D delivery, but they work in unison and can report to the same manager (usually the CEO, COO, CTO, or CPO). Some of the most innovative companies nowadays have senior product leaders with a technological background, such as Shopify and Stripe.

How Do You Evangelize Your Technological Value Externally?

It can be extremely valuable for some companies to have a senior leader as the company's technological "face." This person can help create partnerships and collaborations by finding leverage points and helping clarify the technical sense. They often need to be savvy enough to develop creative solutions for possible problems on the spot and break through any obstacles.

The same can apply to working with high-caliber prospects and clients and striking design partnerships. A rising number of today's "unicorns" have a technical cofounder spend time with clients to find opportunities to add more value and uncover targets for innovation and disruption.

Especially for companies that sell technical products, such as platforms and online services, it can be useful to have a senior executive that actively evangelizes the company in its industry. Think about the kind of person you'd like to have speaking on conference stages on behalf of your company and brushing shoulders with relevant thought leaders and prospects.

How Do You Maximize Tech Leverage Internally?

The other side of the coin from the previous question is ensuring that technology is used to its fullest potential within your ranks. Just as customers can rarely tell what tech solutions they need, the same frequently applies to other departments in your company. A tech team that's attentive to its colleagues can provide a lot more than merely setting up IT systems.

When product and tech people make an effort to find opportunities in-house, they can create an incredible impact that I often refer to as "internal superpowers." Think about tools that save your salespeople hours every day, make marketing campaigns have a better ROI, or make customer support more productive. These all have the chance of significantly improving the company's performance without even considering direct tech work for your customers.

MAPPING RESPONSIBILITIES TO TITLES

Let it be clear: I do not think titles mean as much as they used to a decade ago. The "Chief Technology Officer" (CTO) title has become a catch-all umbrella, with individuals filling completely different roles between companies. Therefore, I highly recommend that you do your expectation-setting with candidates regarding the responsibilities you need help with, as defined above. They should be used in your job descriptions and interviewing processes.

Nevertheless, we live in a society with some standards and therefore cannot easily escape the use of these titles. To help you better attract suitable types of candidates in the first place, here are the most common titles along with their responsibilities.

The Different Types of Tech Executives

Figure 2.1 shows a rough approximation for which titles tend to be used given certain focus areas. The axes show the focus going from entirely internal to the company to external and the "altitude" from tech vision and strategy to implementation and execution.

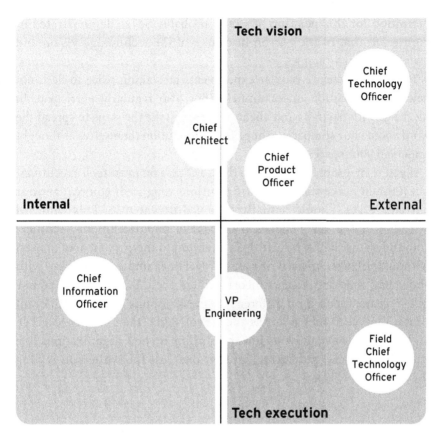

FIGURE 2.1
Roles and their areas of focus.

Chief Technology Officer

The nebulous CTO title is the vaguest. I have seen executives with this title doing the same role as any of the other titles covered below. Therefore, using it can be a double-edged sword. On the one hand, it can be useful as a wildcard to find your first tech executive. On the other hand, it is incredibly easy to make mistakes during the expectation-setting stages of interviewing or confuse other company executives.

The CTO title ostensibly has a specific meaning, but it can genuinely be shaped into whatever you need it to be. It is often donned by cofounders of startups who use it freely without considering its relation to their de facto roles. However, if we think about the "idealized" definition for this position, it would probably be, as demonstrated in Figure 2.1, that of the person in charge of the technology vision and usually outward-facing.

These CTOs ensure regular experiments are taking place to flesh out new tech disruption opportunities. They also regularly participate in meetings with partners and clients and freely take the stage to spread the word about your company, evangelize, and position themselves as thought leaders in your space.

If you're in doubt, you can slap the CTO title on most tech executives, but it might make staffing future positions tougher if you realize your current "CTO" should actually have a different title. This wildcard attribute of the CTO makes it extremely popular among technical cofounders, as they can shift their attention to the current area of need without the hassle of justifying anything. For example, I've worked with about half a dozen Israeli unicorns where the CTOs, over the course of 3–5 years, focused on different business responsibilities at different times. One year they'd act as the VP of R&D, then as a field CTO, and sometimes even invest time in spinning up new organizations like customer success, marketing, and product, all the while still styling themselves as CTOs.

Chief Information Officer

The CIO role is often used at companies that weren't tech-driven from day one. They installed a CIO to be in charge of IT operations, set up some internal tooling, etc. As Figure 2.1 shows, the stereotypical CIO is directed inward at supporting and serving the company's other departments and is often more focused on tactics than strategy.

However, the best CIOs in the industry realize that they have to claim their seat around the boardroom table and therefore are raising their altitude of intervention—to a more strategic role. These leaders in corporates spanning health, insurance, apparel, retail, and, of course, high tech are all focusing on the strategic aspect of their position. In case your technological needs are confined within the company—you will not be selling tech solutions, and they will only be used internally—the CIO might be the right type of executive for you.

SIDEBAR: THE CTO–CIO DIVIDE

Historically, many companies tended to have either a CTO or a CIO, and which one they had would define the company's view of technology. Those committed to using technology as a core part of their strategy would usually have a CTO. Companies that regarded tech as an enabler or service provider would have CIOs. Even though it is not entirely true today, that distinction has created stereotypes that many top tech talents are afraid of: they don't want to work under a CIO.

Therefore, many enterprises now have even multiple CTOs that are not in charge of outward-facing product development as part of their move to embrace technology fully. An example would be Walmart, which mainly uses technology in-house. Along with its doubling down on tech and staffing thousands of tech positions yearly, it is transitioning from having a CIO to having multiple CTOs.

Chief Product Officer

Relatively newer than the previous two, this is part of the understanding that if a company is developing tech products for its customers, it should view product leadership as a critical part of its executive team. This head of product should be in charge of translating the company's strategy and goals into product initiatives. For example, their efforts include nurturing relationships with clients to gain feedback and insights as well as performing product discovery.

Some companies have the R&D organization report to the Chief Product Officer (CPO). The primary heuristic I use to assert whether this makes sense is to consider how much healthy tension is needed in the company between product and R&D. Some companies have a culture where it is less crucial, especially when the CPO is enough technologically savvy to objectively evaluate demands from both sides. Sometimes, when this executive is technical enough, an even newer title is used: the Chief Product and Technology Officer (CPTO).

Vice President of Engineering

When we want someone to lead the tech team and be in charge of the people, processes, and delivery, we usually use a title such as VP R&D or VP

Engineering. Be aware that this should not mean a "junior CTO." People in these roles in bigger organizations often find these responsibilities alone to be enough to fill their time—let alone also evangelizing, for example.

As Figure 2.1 shows, these roles don't have to be limited to focusing either externally or internally, as the work is relatively the same in both cases. These executives should, at the least, be momentum-makers. When their organizations operate smoothly, progress is made regularly and with visible results. The best in these roles avoid a myopic view that centers solely around execution. They inject habitual innovation into their teams' day-to-day operations.

Other Common Roles

There are other roles that are not as widely used but still relatively common and that you should at least have knowledge of.

Chief Architect: A misleading title. I'd estimate only about half of those donning this style are genuinely part of the C-suite. This role is usually focused on the technical aspects of the work. Nevertheless, when staffed with a talented leader, it can vastly help growing tech companies maintain their momentum and create a technological "moat." In such scenarios, it definitely warrants an executive responsibility.

Field CTO: A technological executive that is focused on outward-facing work and evangelism. These positions can often rapidly accelerate sales cycles and create better client and partner relationships with improved expectation setting due to the ability to "talk shop" with counterparts.

Head of Research: A person in charge of creative work that is usually not as straightforward as merely implementing defined features. This can include analyzing data, spotting opportunities to introduce machine learning, and researching technological or business-domain aspects to create established processes and patterns to handle business problems. Sometimes it is part of the purview of the aptly named VP of Research & Development.

Head of Innovation: Some companies resort to introducing tech innovation and creativity by putting a specific person in charge of it. While I've personally helped such endeavors in the past to great success, I still believe that this is not a recommended long-term solution. It encapsulates the permission to use one's creativity in a single department instead of demanding it be treated as part of the job for all technical staff.

SIDEBAR: THE SENIORITY DIAL

In the above, I've used the most frequent title for a specific role, but as with any other role, their seniority can be dialed up and down. For example, some companies have a VP of Technology instead of a CTO, while others prefer an SVP Engineering, EVP Engineering, or even a Chief Engineering Officer. It's also common practice in startups to bring in someone with the title of Director of Engineering, for example, and have that person progress with time and experience (e.g., the director becomes "Head of" becomes "VP of").

This concept also makes it possible to "layer" executives and internal organizations as your company grows. Keep this in mind, and refrain from handing out C-level titles unless the candidate has a brilliant track record. Hiring for potential and growth can work, but ensure that the title reflects this expectation.

HOW MANY TECH LEADERS DOES IT TAKE TO CREATE MARKET DOMINANCE?

After reading this, you might be worried about your next steps. Do not worry. You do not need to put all of these in place as a first step. If you already have some tech executives, it might be a good exercise to answer the business questions above to see where your needs are and compare that to the responsibilities they are currently focusing on. That might help you realize a specific addition that can benefit your company.

If you're just starting out, no one will recommend installing a battery of executives on day one. Instead, you can use these guiding directions to decide on your first hire:

- Are your technological needs currently aimed solely internally? Consider starting with a CTO.

- Do you want to develop a product that's going to be used by customers? Setting up a skeleton for a product engineering organization with a VP of Engineering and VP of Product might be a better decision (sometimes, you can find a person that can do both).
- For technological products, even those exposed to customers, you might be able to start solely with a VP of Engineering.

As explained above, you can use the "seniority dial" to reduce the risk of these first hires. If, after considering this, you are still unsure, getting external expert help to decide on your first steps and aid in the interviewing and staffing process can greatly increase your chances of success.

ACTION ITEMS

Perform a quick assessment to determine your tech leadership's health:

- Consider the different responsibilities and roles required by a tech executive and determine how that should look in your company.
- Compare that ideal scenario to your current situation and point out the differences that need to be improved.
- Honestly assess whether you and the rest of the executive team have provided enough power to your tech leadership.
- Decide on steps forward to tackle the differences you've outlined, which can be as simple as having an expectation-setting meeting or requiring steps like hiring the right people or getting external help.

NOTE

1. Angus Loten, "CIO Role in Flux as Businesses Embrace Tech," *Wall Street Journal*, February 24, 2022. https://www.wsj.com/articles/cio-role-in-flux-as-businesses-embrace-tech-11645705801.

3

Defensive Technology: The Fallacy of Digital Transformations

No work on the current state of tech in enterprises can be complete without addressing the elephant in the room, which is digital transformations. One of the hottest buzzwords around, digital transformation (DT) is perhaps better referred to as a wooly mammoth. There's no doubt you've heard this term thrown around. You might be already in the process of analyzing what DT means for your company or already have a transformation underway. No matter your situation, this chapter will provide guidance and shortcuts to avoid common pitfalls in these transformations.

WHAT'S A DIGITAL TRANSFORMATION?

"Digital transformation" is the generic term used by organizations or companies that decide to overhaul their tech. It often comprises the automation of manual processes, the introduction of newer systems, and the setup of proper R&D departments. Businesses decide to invest in the adoption of technology to achieve better efficiency, become more innovative and competitive, and generate new forms of value to differentiate themselves.

More and more companies report being in the process of such transformations or intending to kick one off. The COVID-19 pandemic has definitely accelerated the technology adoption rate for many businesses and government bodies and probably propelled the whole industry to fast-forward by a few years.

That's all very high level, but what does a digital transformation actually mean? What does it look like during these transformations? What happens

DOI: 10.4324/9781003358473-3

after it? This is where things get very vague and change considerably between organizations.

The "What Year Is It?"

The most straightforward of all transformations is the one where an institute goes from no technology to decent technology in one fell swoop. This has been the goal of many transformations that started in government agencies and municipalities over the past years, especially since the pandemic rushed things.

The work here mainly falls in the "finally!" camp. The changes are primarily obvious, long time coming, and not exciting. That doesn't make them any less valuable. These frequently form the basic structure of technology in order to keep building on top of it in the future.

Depending on the complexity of these initial steps into the digital realm, many of these transformations see success, at least in their first steps that aim at low-hanging fruit. After all, when you finally set up a web page to track issues, it often doesn't require any innovative technology. It is something your customers are already accustomed to from other vendors.

However, things that seem straightforward from the outside frequently aren't so from the inside. For example, even the seemingly trivial issue tracking system we just mentioned might require significant changes to the way things are done internally. For personnel that aren't tech-literate, the crux of the issue is helping them become so and not just putting the technology in place. Thus, transformations that seem to have started delivering value quickly start lagging, which catches leadership teams by surprise.

The Overhaul

A different scenario is where a significant portion of the existing solutions is scrapped in favor of the new and shiny way of doing things. The danger of such grand and sweeping changes is that they tend to look simpler than they really are. We see the existing solution and figure we've already done it once; how complicated will it be to do it again, only using modern tools?

However, when we get going, we see that things are not as easy as they seemed. That is how we repeatedly get airlines, online stores, or government offices that tout a "whole new website" happily but whose users bemoan the change has just made things worse. As a rule of thumb, a business that has to reach an "overhaul" situation has neglected ongoing maintenance and renovations. Therefore, it has reached the point where nothing was possible except for demolishing the whole thing and starting from the ground up.

These sorts of endeavors are likely to go over budget and whoosh by deadlines time and again. It is significantly harder to replace a working system with a lot of complexity baked in and whose users have acclimated to it. Such changes require clear and immediate benefits, or you will face your users' wrath. A few years ago, Hertz initiated an overhaul of its website and apps with Accenture. That digital transformation was never delivered. About 18 months after the initial due date, Hertz finally had it and filed a lawsuit to get back the $32 million it had paid.[1] This is not a rare occurrence, even when some of the most reputable companies in the world are involved.

BACK TO THE FUTURE

A major digital transformation project was initiated during my service in one of the Israeli Defense Force's cyber units. The best, most senior, most talented people were moved to it. Its budget was sizable for our unit. The goal was to revamp older systems to move to new technologies deemed "the right thing." After a year of considering options and vendors, a Fortune 50 software giant was chosen to lead the project.

A couple more years went by. Nothing was delivered. In the meantime, the tech landscape continued evolving at a rapid pace. Eventually, the planned project, which has yet to provide anything, was already becoming obsolete. It was ultimately scrapped, after considerable time, money, and efforts were gone. If this can happen at such a wellspring of talent, innovation, and tech-savvy—the factory of the Startup Nation—it can happen to anyone.

Overhauls are also different in that they come to replace existing technology. Therefore, they have another thing going for them at first glance: the organization isn't really "transforming" but just renewing itself. However, technology has been compared to luxury experiences: it takes very little time for us to get used to it and take it for granted. In a way, even technology that looked cutting-edge a decade ago can seem old and obsolete today. That means that your existing tech chops and solutions, if left unattended to gather dust, have less value nowadays, much like a checking account left behind by inflation.

The Dead Letter Transformation

These are the worst types of initiatives. These are transformations that are not being pursued wholeheartedly and therefore never stood a chance of delivering genuine value. Such a transformation often ensues because of politics. Different departments want to be able to tout how they are cutting-edge or maintain a certain facade of modernity but are not frankly interested in changing their ways.

Whenever such grandiose projects are created without the will to integrate technology with the business truly, it shows in the organization that results. These companies might have an appearance of new technology and an air of sophistication. Still, the detachment from technology means that this wasn't genuinely a transformation, but something more similar to the teenager that quickly cleans up a room before parents are due to be back. Things look ok, ostensibly, but the heaps of clothes hastily shoved into the closet are going to unravel when it's time to change outfits.

Similarly, these lukewarm and lackluster projects result in newly forged tech silos, the same ones other companies try to eliminate through transformations. I am going to believe that if you're spending your time reading this book, you are not interested in embarking on a similar project. However, it is vital to know to spot these so that you can recognize which examples, recommendations, and advisors to avoid.

A TYPICAL TRANSFORMATION LIFECYCLE

Let's assume that Acme Corp has realized it must join the technological revolution and therefore has decided to start a transformation. Strategically, it is clear that it needs to be done, and budgets will be made available. What happens then?

Analysis and Planning

More often than not, merely kicking off a digital transformation is a considerable project in and of itself. Companies that have long been out of the game have a lot of learning to do. Combine that with the high stakes given the significance of such a change on the company's future, as well as the hefty cost, and you get a project that most who are in charge of are more concerned with not messing it up than actually imagine what success would look like.

Thus ensues a months-long analysis marathon. Needs are collected from all over the company. Customers are put in groups and focused upon. Many vendors are approached, and quotes are offered. The nature of this process often prompts leadership to ensure the transformation will encompass as much as possible. No one in their right mind would like to go through this again.

Finally, a vendor is chosen after going back and forth on countless proposals, suggesting roadmaps, and haggling over prices and timelines. Alternatively, in case the company already has a tech department it is often in charge of creating a roadmap and proposal that is accepted and deemed trust-worthy.

Initiation

Whoever was chosen, be it an external vendor or your tech department, now has to kick off the work. Given the fact that it often requires talent that doesn't currently exist in the company, time to onboard external workers (or hire new employees) goes by. During this phase, some companies also manage to start mapping out certain areas in depth to make things ready for work once the required personnel is made available.

Once the team is in place, it gets to work. More often than not, this group will operate in relative solitude. Especially with external suppliers, it is easy to treat the entire team as a foreign object and therefore communicate solely through a handful of defined points of contact. Even with in-house IT and tech departments, it is easy to continue treating them as the silos they've been before. Adhering to Conway's law,[2] this forms the frame for the entire project's success from the get-go.

Execution

At this point, work ensues at full speed. Nevertheless, timelines are mind-boggling given the big goals and the tendency to add to these projects everything and the kitchen sink. In the Hertz example earlier, the new website was initially planned to go live about 18 months after kickoff.

When not managed properly, these grand goals lend themselves to working in big bites, meaning that no tangible result is visible for months on end. As the team is doing its best, things inevitably change. Perhaps the company has decided to shift its strategy. Maybe a geopolitical event requires a certain pivot. It could be as simple as realizing that some details were overlooked; therefore, the approach should be tweaked.

Some changes are deemed no longer feasible or worthwhile, as they would require too much effort. Others are incorporated into the existing plan, often requiring formal "change requests," updated timelines, and increased budgets. All the while, the lack of visibility means that virtually no one in the company can tell how well the effort is going and whether it is still on track.

The Real World

In the end, something happens. Sometimes the transformation is declared as successful or, at least, completed. This means that the bulk of the work has been performed, and the business can put those efforts to use.

However, nothing in life is constant, and neither will a newly fangled solution remain correct in eternity. Changes, improvements, and corrections will be required constantly. At the very least, there's essential maintenance. Even without attempting to add any new capabilities, tech requires an effort to keep working. For example, operating systems and hardware change regularly, and the software needs to be adapted to support them. App stores regularly announce new rules, often for privacy and compatibility, that require companies to dust off most apps regularly.

Sometimes, in our rush to get the transformation out the door, we cut some of the initial scope. That means that there are needs that we are aware of and that should continue to be developed, even as the bulk of the transformation has been made public already. This might happen using the same team or a smaller one.

Moreover, even a flawlessly executed transformation process cannot foretell the future. A genuine transformation means that technology should constantly adapt and innovate, just like the rest of your business. Therefore, it should not be left to become stale but continuously worked on.

When the value generated from these ongoing efforts is clear and visible, it can often induce more significant technological investments. This might be the best indicator of successful integration of technology: we double down on it not out of necessity but because it pays off.

WHY TRANSFORMATIONS FAIL

Having covered how transformations frequently look, it is important to highlight the issues with this model. After all, failed and over budget, projects are estimated to lose businesses billions and billions every year. Looking at each step of the cycle and appraising your team on which pitfalls they contain will help ensure your success.

Ill-Conceived Beginning

A considerable portion of the problems in these projects can be traced back directly to issues with their conception. During the analysis and planning stage, we tend to make these mistakes.

Thinking too small: Especially for companies that lack a tech visionary, it can be very hard to imagine what technology can provide the company. The obvious steps are easy to plan and find help with, but what about the genuinely innovative parts? When a typical transformation project takes a couple of years at minimum, it can be easy to only consider what is needed and straightforward right now without taking into account how the technology landscape might look by that time.

That is how we often release a brand new app that already feels outdated. Another example is when a particular technological solution is chosen at kickoff because it seems to be used throughout the industry. However, that solution turns out to have been in its "midlife." While still usable, it is losing its market share. By the time the product is made available, it is no longer the recommended way of doing things.

Thinking too big: There's no real problem with thinking big. That is actually what technology is best for. However, we should keep in mind that the bigger the initial scope is, the greater the risks of running over budget and missing deadlines, as well as for the industry and market conditions to change during the transformation's execution. Therefore, to run a successful transformation, you have the challenge of trying to find the Goldilocks sweet spot that works for your company's situation.

Projects that are too big tend to be treated as binary. They either succeed, or they fail. With the innate risks of big change initiatives, this is akin to a coin toss. Thinking big but still managing to chunk the effort into reasonable milestones can make all the difference.

Geek deficiency: As discussed in the previous chapter, embracing tech with both arms means that you need a solid tech leadership team to take charge of any significant initiative. Digital transformations started without a strong executive and a capable team to back and accompany the project are a lot less likely to fulfill their potential.

This doesn't mean such projects should never be done with outsourcing help or agencies. Merely that even those, with all of their experience, should be accompanied by in-house expertise that lives and breathes your company's situation, market, and interests. Otherwise, these projects are often treated as disconnected side projects that are never sincerely integrated with the rest of the company. That's hardly what a transformation should mean.

Weak Kickoffs

The initiation phase suffers from similar problems.

The fortress of solitude: First and most important is the propensity to kick off the project in solitude. The relevant personnel might start collecting requirements and asking for more details, but this is done as vendors rather than as collaborators or partners. The supplier-like mentality is an issue even when an external agency does not lead the project. This sets the stage for how communication will happen throughout the process. Therefore, it solidifies the problems that Conway's law introduces and limits collaboration.

Rigid processes: You can tell that this is happening when the discussion revolves around nailing down processes and defining "handoffs" or "sign-offs." While ostensibly looking like the establishment of a working relationship, this process focus is, in all truth, a rouse to avoid genuine cooperation.

Whom do we define rigid processes and "verbal contracts" with? Surely not with peers, teammates, and collaborators. Thus, letting the initiation stage take place in this manner guarantees a standoffish relationship from day one. While it might seem like a rigid requirement for some larger organizations to have such processes defined, you should still exercise common sense. When enterprises tout an initiative as an "internal startup," the best indicator I know of whether this is genuine or merely lip service is if communication across all actors is open and collaborative. After all, that is a major part of the magic of startups.

The Sausage Factory

While the problems of prior stages can be subtler to note, it is easier to spot these pitfalls in the execution phase. That aids us, but do keep in mind that many of these can stem from mistakes performed earlier, and thus handling even the issues you can spot now is already failure work.

Capricious changes: As the transformation behemoth slowly starts on its path, we are bound to encounter surprises. Every so often, there are distractions along the road, and companies frequently get sucked into following whatever craze *du jour* they think about. Changing course too rapidly—especially when disconnected from any more comprehensive strategy that aids in making these shifts and aligns the entire team around the changes—is like quicksand for projects. It leads to death by busy work.

It's not that anyone is idly sitting and not doing anything. On the contrary, I've seen teams burning the midnight oil yet achieve nothing of significance. That's because they never continue on a path long enough to reach a destination. These Groundhog Day projects end up taking much longer and can sometimes accelerate burnout across the team.

Sacred rigidity: By this point, you've no doubt grasped that any extreme is a bad idea, and the same applies to changes. Just as too many changes are determined, so are too few. Some transformations are led with such bureaucratic fervor for "following the plan" that no change, however small, is easy to make. While some discipline is required to avoid the previous pitfall, too much is just as bad. To continue the path analogy from earlier, it is like seeing that the path leads to a dead-end and continuing forward nevertheless because "the map says so."

Especially given the sheer amount of changes the tech industry sees every quarter, and the ambiguity the global economy has been through since 2020, it makes little sense to treat plans as if they were set in stone. Your company needs a strategy to help make tactical decisions effectively, but even the strategy should be revisited and perhaps revised once every 12–18 months.

Therefore, transformations that span years will definitely have to adapt as they go. There is no reason to miss out on possible innovations or fail to seize a business opportunity solely to avoid changing the plan. Everything should be considered from the point of view of return on investment and whether the detour or course change make sense.

Lack of feedback: A direct result of the silo approach discussed in the previous steps is that the transformation team keeps on its work merrily without meriting any consideration from the rest of the company. Sometimes it is because the team doesn't create transparency and demo its progress. Other times, business leadership is disinterested. It could also be an amalgam of both. No matter the reason, the result is that work is being done and not reviewed properly.

Therefore, when the team inevitably goes off track and does something wrong, it will be spotted too late (note that I say "when." There's no doubt that such things will happen). Feedback is crucial to ensure that what is being performed answers the business needs and quickly discover when the work is suboptimal, irrelevant, or overengineered.

The latter is when the solution is much better and more elaborate than is required to achieve the end goal. It is kind of like what happens when I insist on purchasing a fully specced and upgraded MacBook Pro, even though I no longer code for a living. The computer is going to work, but I probably could have made do with a cheaper model. When we allow ourselves to gold-plate features and projects—the term for overly perfect or engineered projects—we let our egos dictate the work.

Disconnect from the market: Sometimes, the focus on the transformation drains the company from the ability to do anything else. This starvation of other parts of the business, particularly any tech-related matters, can spiral out of hand. This then introduces more stress to the transformation, as the effects take their toll on the bottom line, and a vicious cycle can be introduced. The focus is solely on the transformation, hurting other parts, which makes everyone more anxious about getting things done fast, which in turn makes them go heads down and focus on the transformation even more.

There's an Israeli company, whose name I'll leave out, that has created a tool that is so common in daily use for Israeli companies and freelancers that its name is often used as the general term for the product (kind of like my parents say they're "Googling" something whenever they use a search box, no matter where). Though focused on a single small niche, this was a beloved product for years. They recently decided to aim higher, which is not a bad thing. The process, however, was lacking. As a client, I could see more and more bugs being introduced, and the quality was deteriorating. More and more customers started to complain online. Once their big transformation was completed and announced, rather than have everyone rave about it, their old clients were commenting with sorrow about the product they once loved. Long transformations cannot be done while neglecting the rest of the business.

A Long-Expected Party

When things are all set up and finally ready to be used, there is often a lot of commotion. However, as the awaited solution goes live and finally meets the real world, there are mistakes both in the going-live process itself and afterward.

Pulling Band-Aid: Sometimes, there is a great rush to get the finished product in people's hands as fast as possible. That desire leads to things happening haphazardly, without due process, and lowering risks. This is especially the case for transformations that have exceeded their budgets and deadlines. Due to that, they are all the more eager to finally be "done."

Keeping this eagerness in mind, it does not make sense to try and pull the switch on a grand change in one go when the stakes are high. Things should be done gradually, in a way that allows us to monitor whether issues are emerging and tackle them before they affect the business too much. Big Bang rollouts are needlessly risky.

Poor communication: Those in the company who were immersed knee-deep in the transformation project for years frequently have difficulty visualizing how things are seen from the outside. Therefore, when there comes the time to introduce the project to new users, either external or internal, they fail to do so in a way that maximizes their chances of success. How many times did you suddenly get an email from a SaaS you use that touted a whole slew of changes that you weren't expecting?

I can't even remember the number of times I opened my browser to use a tool I've been using for years only to suddenly see unexpected changes. Now, instead of doing what I intended to do, I need to shave a few yaks before I can (hopefully) get back on track.[3] As with any project, proper communication is crucial for success. Otherwise, your users won't use your product, grok the improvements it offers, or take the time to utilize it fully. Instead, you might arouse ire and discontent. When this occurs, projects that were supposed to evolve the company end up devolving it.

Now you see me, now you don't: Lastly, when technology hasn't really been embraced—especially when the working team is mainly or wholly external—it can result in an orphaned project once it is released. Even when the contracts come with some ongoing maintenance and support, those tend to be reserved for urgent needs or done in concentrated efforts once a quarter.

Given the highly variable nature of technology, along with the minuscule chances that whatever initial version that was released also happened to be the perfect one, the users and customers might feel abandoned. At the beginning of the *Lord of the Rings*, Bilbo invited everyone to a big party and then disappeared, leaving the guests baffled. Too often, we do the same when we allow transformations to come to a complete standstill.

RIGHTING THE SHIP

Regardless of whether you've already embarked on such a complex transformation or are merely considering one, you can make things better. At the core, this starts with performing this with the right mindsets and objectives. Trying to don technology and secure it to your organization with duct tape will obviously not cut it.

This stems from applying technology defensively. Companies that fear missing out or that want to appear modern. Executives that read something and are trying to copy-and-paste it to their roles without the needed adjustments. Success is possible solely for those who genuinely embrace technology and wield it as a strategic factor.

To set yourself for success, evaluate your existing or planned projects with the best practices laid out in the previous chapters, and assess whether you have gained alignment.

Figure 3.1 shows that we can attempt to reach the same destination in entirely different ways. Too often, transformations are performed as some sort of tight-rope act. There are no tangible ways to stop in the middle or change course. It's done almost blindfold because there are silos and severe gaps in communication. The end goal isn't even well defined, and without any guidance, you'll have to feel around with your feet. Well-executed

FIGURE 3.1
Different paths of transformations.

transformations, on the other hand, are radically different. They create bite-sized (or the enterprise equivalent of these) goals. We can see where we are and evaluate our path forward at each step along the way. We have leaders helping guide the way, and there is always a clear goal within sight. Not much of a choice.

Tech as a Strategy

The essential part of any successful transformation, whether starting from scratch or evolving, is ensuring that your leadership team is committed to technology becoming a central part of your business. Therefore, the projects should align with the company's strategy for the years to come. Even better is to revise your strategy with technology in mind and only then kick off the right projects.

This means that you should have solid tech expertise in-house, at least for the project's leadership. Those leaders should have adequate power and autonomy. These geeks in the boardroom are crucial for most bridging work between the tech force and the rest of the business. Such executives who are privy to the strategy, roadmap, and high-impact consideration can help maintain a healthy connection between the project and the business's needs.

Moreover, as with every strategy, you should have a defined vision that you are moving toward. The strategy is a means to get closer to making that vision a reality. Simply stating what strategic work is to be done is not enough. All tech efforts should be weighed against the grand vision to ensure they genuinely get you closer to it. Some things that look helpful initially are really only expensive detours.

Assessment questions:

- Was your strategy recently refreshed with a focus on how to best leverage technology?
- Do you have senior tech leaders to rely on?
- Are those leaders involved enough and have the proper context to make the right decisions?
- What is your goal? What would be considered a success?

Internalizing R&D

As we saw, many of the issues in these projects can be attributed to poor organizational structures that beget detachment, politics, and bureaucracy. Your R&D efforts cannot be put in a silo or left aside. Integrate the work with the rest of the business.

When working with outsourcing or external companies to execute these initiatives, this is always harder to achieve. That is not to say that it is bad or shouldn't happen. If you've considered all options and find this is the right path forward, go ahead. However, be aware of this disadvantage and work actively to negate it.

There should be many continuous communication streams between the tech people and the rest of the company. Ideally, even when working with external help, you should have a small in-house team to direct them. Rather than attempting to define strict "handoffs" and touch points, make collaboration flexible and ongoing. Creating cross-functional teams might be a bit tough initially for individuals, but it can do wonders to speed projects along.

Assessment questions:

- Are you taking into consideration Conway's law?
- Is communication strictly defined and limited to allowed channels, consists of specific templates, and mainly done through online systems? Is that what teamwork means at your company?
- Would conversations between both sides—outside of defined rituals—seem strange or surprising? That is a clear sign of bad communication culture.

Create a Business Connection

Another vital aspect for any tech team, especially during big transformations, is ensuring an always present sense of urgency. This is an urgency to deliver, create an impact, and improve the clients' condition. Do not confuse this with stressing the team out.

Instead, this is about sharing goals and objectives with the team so that it can grasp what it is attempting to achieve. It also entails constant vigilance to ensure that we do not cut ourselves too much slack in our cycles. When teams understand the meaning of their work, they are more likely to be driven to get these results faster, as well as see the importance of fast feedback cycles that ensure that they remain on track.

This generates a drive for impact, decreasing the chances of useless work being done. When done from the project's inception, it also often results in healthy milestones and iterations being baked into the timeline. That provides maximal flexibility—as there are more options to change course—as well as invites more priceless feedback.

We want those doing the work to see its impact on the clients. They should hear how customers are happy with what they got or which issues are troubling them. That makes them more likely to get their sense of achievement from driving even more impact instead of letting shiny technology blind them.

Assessment questions:

- In discussions, is the conversation revolving around technical details, or does the team understand the goal and speaks in product terms?
- How are you exposing the team to the results of their work?
- How much of a sense of urgency do you feel there is to get to the market and get the product in people's hands?

DOING IT RIGHT: TARGET'S TRANSFORMATION

After seeing all the examples of failed transformations, I thought you would appreciate an example that shows it can be done successfully. I like Target's story because it shows that there is no such thing as a perfect or flawless transformation, yet success can be substantial.

It seems that initially, Target's leadership didn't grasp the importance of technology for its future.[4] For a few years, their online orders system was outsourced to Amazon! Target, now directly in competition with Amazon, was so disinterested in tech advancements that it let its competitor take charge of it.

Eventually, they realized that technology had to become genuinely integrated. That wasn't simple. There were a few crashes in the first few weeks after Target took over its websites. Nevertheless, they slowly made more progress, and Target found its footing.

Target made a genuine commitment. That can be easily seen externally. For example, they have a Chief Digital Officer and a cadre of tech executives and leaders. They are investing in R&D amounts that show that this is more than mere lip service—they want to innovate. And they're getting their money's worth: since this began, Target's stock price has soared. Digital revenue grew from small percentages to roughly 20% of total revenue and is increasing even in bad quarters.[5]

ACTION ITEMS

Successful transformations are not easy to pull off and require the cooperation of all involved. However, by following the principles above and being mindful of the common pitfalls and bad practices, you are already poised at the top 10% for such projects.

- If you haven't yet, refresh your strategy with a tech-driven (or, at the very least, very tech-enabled) perspective. Gone are the days where strategies required months of work and comprised dozens of pages no one ever read. You should renew yours every 12–18 months. Practicing Sentient Strategy® with my clients often takes just a couple of days of work.
- Synchronize your executive team and tech leadership about these concepts as the baseline for any endeavor.
- Ensure that your leadership team is tech-literate. More on that in the next chapter.
- Whether you have an existing project underway or are initiating one, introduce the concept of time-to-value for every step and minimize radio silence.

NOTES

1. https://www.henricodolfing.com/2019/10/case-study-hertz-accenture-website.html.
2. "Any organization that designs a system (defined broadly) will produce a design whose structure is a copy of the organization's communication structure." https://en.wikipedia.org/wiki/Conway%27s_law
3. Yak shaving is used to describe seemingly useless work that's very remote from what you set out to do, but that, for some obscure reason, is required to get to your objective.
4. Target Transforms for the Digital Age, HBS. https://digital.hbs.edu/platform-digit/submission/target-transforms-for-the-digital-age/.
5. Target's online sales grow $13 billion over 2 years, Digital Commerce 360. https://www.digitalcommerce360.com/2022/03/03/target-online-sales-grow-13-billion-over-2-years/.

4

Forging Cyborgs: Assimilating Tech Throughout Your Ranks

Having gone through the trouble of explaining the importance of putting great tech leadership in place, we should ensure that the other parties are also aligned. It takes two to tango, and even the best and brightest tech leaders can't guarantee impact without cooperation from their peers. And from your leadership, the same mindset should trickle down to the entire organization.

TECHNIFYING EXECUTIVES

Even though you should have dedicated tech executives, you shouldn't stop there. All your executives and senior leaders should embrace technology as part of their arsenal. Depending on their background, experience, and mindset, this can require different approaches. You might be surprised to hear that these aren't intimidating or scary, nor do they require your leadership team to "geek up" (not that there's anything wrong with that).

Explaining Tech

First and foremost, for some leaders, the concept of modern R&D might be foreign. Even for someone that's worked in high-tech before, working in an enterprise software business can be very different than operating a modern SaaS. Therefore, all your senior leaders should go through a basic "onboarding" orientation where they learn what technology means specifically for your company.

DOI: 10.4324/9781003358473-4

Your tech executives should lead this process. That way, it ensures that both sides start forming relationships from day one. Having to hold such a session in the form of an orientation—or basic introduction—also guarantees that the language used will be appropriate. The tech people are less likely to throw a bunch of jargon around in such instances. This is a worthwhile exercise even for your current executives, in case they never went through a similar onboarding.

The measure of success for such a program should be that those who go through it have a basic understanding of the R&D team's structure, its responsibilities, and how to best cooperate with it, along with forming initial relationships with key personnel. The agenda should include these items:

- Overview of the R&D organization's structure and basic explanations for the types of responsibilities different titles hold. This is specifically important for those who are not used to the myriad titles used by software engineering ICs and managers. I've often seen people confused about the difference between Tech Leads and Team Leads or who should be contacted when there is a problem with a particular product.
- An explanation of what the typical work cycle looks like. In most well-run organizations, there are a few cadences in different altitudes. Therefore, there are more appropriate times to introduce requests and changes. For an outsider, tech teams that reject most requests with an honest explanation that they are "in the middle of a sprint" don't mean a lot. However, suppose they learn how the cadence works, how to inject their agendas, and how the prioritization works. In that case, they gain a mental model for the organization that they can use to collaborate more effectively.
- An introduction to the current roadmap, the objectives, how they are measured, and the key people responsible for them. Assuming that R&D's objectives are connected to real business needs, each executive will probably need to be in touch with certain teams.
- A feedback request: each executive should know what type of feedback is most useful for their cooperation with R&D. For example, the head of Customer Success can provide the team with insights about technical issues that don't reach the engineers usually, as customer success specialists address them. Helping the R&D team peer into its blind spots immediately ensures that the relationship is valuable for both sides.

The main takeaway should be that this orientation is not intended to make them part of the team but merely capable of understanding how the R&D department operates and how to collaborate with it. This effort should help make the "others" into real people, thus allowing more genuine and effective communication.

Creating an Executive *Team*

With the basic introductions out of the way, the company's senior leadership's role is to ensure the executive team acts like a team. It is very easy to form cliques within this team where the business folks only talk to the tech folks when something has gone wrong. However, that's not nearly good enough and effectively guarantees that communication is solely happening when it is already too late to avoid the mistakes.

Jelling the senior team often starts with the CEO. The different objectives and significant roadmap items should be leveraged for this. If goals don't overlap in responsibility and accountability, silos naturally emerge. Each side ensures that their part is going well, even at the expense of others. This is human nature, and while it might not happen everywhere, it means that extra effort is required to avoid it. Instead, have project OKRs[1] shared between different departments where no side can claim success individually.

This is also exemplified by organizational structures that center around collaboration. Establishing cross-functional teams that have members from different disciplines working together side-by-side innately brings people together, leadership included. Be vigilant about spotting "us vs. them" thinking and nipping it in the bud.

Lastly, when it comes to creating genuine teams, I have always found it worthwhile to ensure that regular touch points are happening. Many executives feel like the last thing they need is another meeting on the calendar. It is perfectly fine to be protective of your time, but not when it means that executives can spend months without exchanging more than a few words. Regular team or one-on-one meetings between peers in the senior leadership team are invaluable.

Staying Current

A relatively easy and straightforward way to connect different departments, especially their leaders, with technology is to ensure they make good use of it. A big part of that is obviously about developments from your R&D team that are part of the more extensive roadmap. However, it shouldn't be limited to that.

Given the rapid pace at which technology is advancing, there is no chance of any single person—or team—keeping up with all developments and changes. Your engineers are likely struggling to ensure that they're still using the best tools for the job and regularly refreshing older parts of the product. Unless they have specific interests or work focus on other areas, they will not be the most updated when it comes to other technologies being developed and offered outside of the company.

That is why every team, and leaders specifically, ought to remain current with technological improvements that might be relevant to them. After all, no one should have a monopoly on technology within the company, and the different departments are certainly not confined to solely using the software developed in-house. These can be big or small. You never know where the next improvement or big leap will come from.

Stand-Alone Tools

The area that is probably easiest to start with and often provides excellent low-hanging fruit is the integration of stand-alone tools. These are services and offerings that professionals can use to make their work better. Some obvious examples include using focused tools for particular tasks and professions completely unrelated to your product.

Salespeople who hear about amazing sales tools like Gong[2] that uses AI to analyze calls and provide coaching automatically should be able to try it immediately. I've yet to see a marketing or content person that has to work on podcasts and videos not completely have their mind blown the first time they see how tools like Descript[3] can save them hours every month. These are the newer tools that everyone should be able to easily check out and play with.

Because these tools are often relatively disconnected from other systems, their integration should be easy and require little effort from your tech department. Of course, IT might have to be involved for permissions and security reasons. Nevertheless, such tinkering should be encouraged. These enhancements might make daily work a bit easier, or they might turn into game changers. The small risk is well worth the potential gains.

Business Software

Of course, there are also the bigger tech integrations that might not even register as innovative technology given how used to them we have become. Sales and marketing teams expect tools like Salesforce to be in place and available. Customer Success can hardly get any work done without industry standards such as Zendesk or Intercom. Growth teams rely on more analytics and tracking tools than I can remember.

These tools can comprise complete operating systems for teams who work within them most of the day. Therefore, their integrations aren't as straightforward and might require ongoing maintenance and experienced engineers. These aren't technologies that can be quickly replaced or overhauled for these reasons. They often require dedicated people's planning and assignment for proof-of-concept projects and updates.

Even though it is more demanding, such initiatives should be encouraged. A good balance is all it takes. It is healthy for each profession to regularly consider the more significant tools it uses to see if it needs an upgrade, an addition, or a replacement.

Product Integrations

One other type of software requires a tight connection with the product. This integration can enrich the information shares across different parts of the organization and enable a better experience for your customers or increase ROI on other fronts. Consider marketing automation tools that send promotional messages at just the right time. Or customer success tools that show more context about a user that is having an issue, so the team best handles it (how many times did you feel like you had to tell some chatbot a lot of stuff it already should have known?).

These integrations can significantly impact the company's bottom line and the efficacy of different departments due to it being more closely coupled with your product. Unfortunately, that is precisely why such integrations are often also relatively expensive to do. Mistakes might expose a lot of sensitive information or even harm the regular operation of your services. Because of that, these are not the sort of technological changes someone makes when they have 30 minutes.

Such strategic use of software cannot be changed every week or even every month. The good news is that your executives are not likely to come across these too often. Ensure that all sides have a healthy relationship that allows them to discuss the benefits, costs, and risks to determine whether it is worth the effort and prioritize it together. A frequent misalignment is that these integrations, while often providing significant ROI and business impact, tend to be viewed as grunt work by the techies.

After all, it is less "sexy" or challenging to integrate with existing tools— which some engineers refer to as "plumbing." For many, it is much more satisfying to write their own solutions and devise clever approaches by themselves. Unfortunately, doing that is a waste. The best way to address this is to make the value very tangible and share the success and credit with the engineers so they feel valuable.

Figure 4.1 shows the common cases for each option. As you can see, there is a clear correlation between the level of effort and the expected gains. Ensure that this is always the case when taking on new projects, and prioritize them with this in mind.

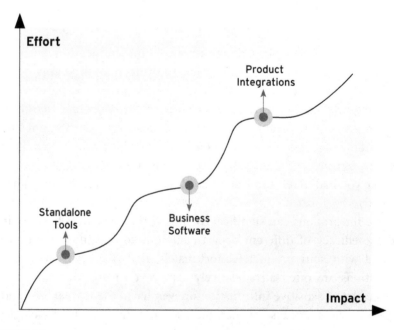

FIGURE 4.1
Different technological solutions and their effort vs. impact.

Being in the Loop

At the end of the day, the bottom line is that executives have a responsibility to remain up to date with things going up in their world. They don't have to do all of it by themselves. It is excellent if others in their departments are involved and are always on the lookout for opportunities or promising products. Nevertheless, this cultural value needs to be modeled by the executives.

By doing that, they help ingrain technology as part of everyone's toolset and reduce mental barriers to considering such options. Is your executive team aware of what others in the industry are doing, talking to vendors, and more? Further, having this knowledge can help ensure that others don't view R&D merely as a cost center. When they become aware of more opportunities and collaborations, R&D moves closer to the coveted innovation center position.

MAKING EMPLOYEES TECH-LITERATE

It should go without saying that capitalizing on technology requires more than a tech-driven (or tech-aware) leadership team. This has to become innate to everyone else to maximize potential. Luckily, doing so is increasingly easy after taking care of the last part. By bringing your leadership team into the fold with tech, they can better lead their teams around these matters.

Teaching Literacy

Tech literacy is a prerequisite for this endeavor. The term *digital literacy* is often used to describe the ability to leverage essential 21st-century tools. For example, being able to type, communicate, search, etc. effectively. I would like to believe that this is a nonissue for most employees in our realm. *Tech literacy* is more than merely being a citizen of a digital world; it comprises the skills needed to work and create using technology.

Employees that lack these skills are often either unaware of the missed benefits of the technology available to them or are intimidated. Both should be tackled as part of your company's culture forming.

The Unknown Unknowns

As always, to make people change, we have to keep in mind *what's in it for them*. Therefore, to help those team members unaware of the improvements they are missing out on, your tech-related training programs should center around making life better for them.

As Donald Rumsfeld said, there are things that we don't know we don't know. It is your responsibility to manifest revelations and make your people enlightened. Create laser-focused guides and walkthroughs that show how they can save time and effort. Is there a way to create reports much faster? Perhaps your existing tools provide a smarter way to prioritize work tasks, prospects, or customer requests in a manner that will make the employee noticeably better. That's always a plus.

Those in charge of these trainings—both as part of onboarding and routine refreshers—should always be actively looking for new nuggets of value. Whenever they spot another trick or productivity hack, they should file it to be shared in the next installment. Those going through the training should feel like they got ahold of precious secrets or gained new superpowers. This is the bar we should have for high-value knowledge transfer.

Lastly, another way to align learning technology with employees' self-interests is to make it a parameter for assessing their performance. When they know embracing the latest method of doing things is also likely to increase their odds of getting promoted, people tend to be more open to innovation.

Disarming Fear

The second part of making people learn new skills and try new technology is to reduce their fear of doing so. Fears might be present due to past mistakes and tools that are not user-friendly and error-prone. I once saw a database administrator (DBA) barge into a room when he noticed a production issue. He quickly looked around and spied two new hires. He then groaned, "You two! You're new. What did you do to the database just now?"

That's not a very warm welcome, and you can see how this would make those employees hesitant ever to touch that system again. In his defense, I'll say that the DBA was right: they were responsible for the problem.

Nevertheless, they cannot be blamed. Sound tech systems are made with their end users in mind. They must be built to prevent likely errors, have checks and balances, and guide users on the right path.

Ensure that every critical system within your company adheres to this principle. Otherwise, you will quickly see people stop using it. After all, no responsible worker would like to risk causing trouble. Additionally, ensure that whenever mistakes do happen, it is treated appropriately. Rather than pointing fingers, the root cause should be determined, and protections should be put in place to prevent similar mistakes from recurring.

Moving beyond Faster Horses

The old adage says that, prior to its invention, people would never have asked for the automobile but instead demanded faster horses. That is due to them not being able to imagine it. People cannot ask for something they cannot even think of. This is similar to the unknown unknowns mentioned earlier. However, this is not about people missing out on what existing tools can do but about asking for new ones.

Part of tech literacy is to ensure that we bestow a broader perspective upon everyone. Throughout your ranks, talented personnel should be capable of envisioning possible approaches. Some of this is established by staying current with technological advancements, as already covered, but this is where your tech team can shine and solidify its connection with others in the company.

At least once a quarter, you should have company-wide show-and-tells with distilled presentations. These talks or summaries should be honed to create "a-ha moments" and broaden the team's horizons. You are not looking for fluff or dry technical talks but something closer to a TED talk. There is no need to go into how things actually work. We want to create a sense of wonder, along with priming the brains in the company to notice other similar opportunities. Priming here means teaching the brain's innate pattern-matching to pay attention to particular types of problems where tech might be helpful.

When smartphones were new, the concept of apps was novel, and we had to be told about specific apps for specific needs. Nowadays, we take their existence for granted and instinctively search for apps to solve a particular need, much like one might search Google for an answer. "There's an app for that" has become a meme. That is only because we have ingrained this technological concept. The same can be done with all tech aspects pertaining to your business. Thus, people will know there are better options than horses with caffeine IVs.

Cross-Pollinate

Another great way of increasing tech literacy throughout your company is cross-pollination between departments—although this means you have to be in it for the long game. Cross-pollination means that positions are staffed by people with experience in different disciplines. Thus, you get the benefit of added depth and easier collaboration.

Having a marketing person that used to be a software engineer means that she'll be able to "talk shop" with R&D and come to them with more ideas. She is also likely to impart wisdom to her teammates during her daily work. For example, as she is going about meetings planning a new project, she might casually mention that there is a shortcut to doing something if the right tech is brought or at a low-effort investment by the engineering department.

Cross-pollination also works great the other way around, where people from different backgrounds enter tech roles. These employees often enable better communication with their counterparts and can aid in connecting their R&D team to the results of what they are doing. Making this a criterion taken into consideration in your hiring and staffing processes is relatively trivial and can have a profound impact over time.

Internal vs. External

When considering how to make this happen, you have two possible options. One is to prioritize external hires that have a multidisciplinary background. A great thing to notice during your regular processes, it is also somewhat of a "unicorn"—rare and often coveted by many potential employers. Ensure that your hiring managers notice this and take it into consideration. Unfortunately, you can rarely rely solely on external and experienced.

For more established organizations, providing internal role mobility is a classic win-win situation. First, for your employees, it directly translates as an invaluable perk if they ever want to change career directions or experiment. While in other companies, they might have to change jobs with all the hassle and risk involved, you can create an environment where such flow between roles is more natural.

Second, if you are able to invest in the mentoring of these employees, your company benefits as well. You gain cross-pollination that goes deeper. Those workers that have "changed teams" still maintain relationships in other parts of the company and come equipped with a different perspective. Done correctly, this is better than hiring inexperienced juniors externally. I witnessed this firsthand when advising Gloat,[4] who are revolutionizing workforces throughout industries by increasing worker mobility and enabling easier upskilling.

CREATE HEALTHY FRICTION

Lastly, your organizational structure should revolve around the touch points between tech and the rest of the business and how to leverage them. This viewpoint is the exact opposite of what many attempt to achieve: clear boundaries and defined procedures. Those unaware of the benefits of tech integration try to minimize the surface area between departments. They couldn't be more wrong.

Product Mastery

When considering the people in your tech people, there are three broad categories of skills that the greats master. First is the *tech mastery*, which refers to how good they are at their craft. This should be relatively straightforward, and if you are reading this book, I will go ahead and assume that it is not an issue. The proper hiring practices, along with swift action when inevitably staffing mistakes occur, take care of most of it.

The second part is *soft skills*, which are vaguer and not as easy to pinpoint. In today's industry, these are also a must for high-performing organizations where individuals are given more leeway and communication happens across different disciplines, mediums, and countries. Soft skills such as clear communication, time management, and decision-making are crucial, and good organizations should ensure that these are actively coached and improved upon by managers.

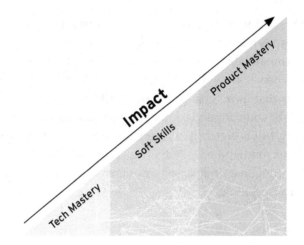

FIGURE 4.2
Rising impact of different skill sets.

The last part is at once both the most impactful and the rarest. This is *product mastery*. Product mastery, similar to tech mastery, refers to the engineers' (and everyone else in the company, really) ability to grasp the different aspects of the company's product, users, market, competition, and more. Because it is unique to every company, every employee has to relearn it, no matter how experienced. It is also constantly evolving and has to be proactively maintained. Figure 4.2 shows the skillsets and their relationship to impact.

Visibility for Mastery

Product mastery is hard to achieve because it requires effort from all sides. Frequently, the need is unclear to those outside of tech, who view the information as trivial. Similarly, the knowledge product mastery is composed of is dismissed by engineers when we do not make it clear how impactful it can be on their performance and ability to leverage their position in the company.

Thus, your executive team has to operate a two-handed maneuver here. The first is about making crucial product-related knowledge accessible to everyone in the company, and specifically your R&D organization. This gradual process starts from an essential organizational skill: creating visibility.

Visibility means we take information, resources, and feedback and make them accessible. Doing so requires understanding our limitations. Mainly, that both parties—those who are sharing the knowledge and those we expected to use it—are short on time as it is. Thus, this effort has to be done with attention to the return on investment. No one should produce towering reports and compilations of all there is to know. That would be an abysmal waste of time.

When helping companies dramatically increase their product mastery, I've found it helpful to start by asking managers throughout the organization to be mindful of relevant tidbits and sharing these as concentrated "insight-bombs." For example, the salespeople can release a five-minute clip every month of the most common reactions prospects have to the product and new features, so everyone else can see how users talk about the problem. Customer Success might set up a newsletter or Slack channel with great (or bad) reviews. Product leaders, who should always be attuned to the industry and market changes, can hold "state of the industry" sessions once a quarter.

The other part of creating product mastery is ensuring that R&D realizes its importance and strives to gain it. This ought to be one of the tenets of R&D's culture and a value that is pursued.[5] For more resources about gaining product mastery see *The Tech Executive Operating System.*

As Figure 4.3 shows, visibility provides the basis. With time, as R&D (and everyone else) get more of this friction in their day-to-day work, it slowly morphs from abstract concepts to something more concrete. As awareness forms, engineers keep in mind certain business aspects that need to be accounted for in their work. Then, acquaintance is reached

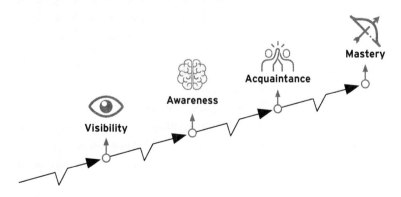

FIGURE 4.3
Working toward product mastery.

when they begin to anticipate certain requirements or problems before those arise, merely due to this familiarity with the broader context.

Eventually, product mastery is reached. At this stage, the tech team is capable of poking holes in planned features and suggesting better approaches. Every moment spent coding has significantly more impact. This holy grail is within grasp, but it requires cooperation and devotion by all parties.

WORKING ON WIDGETS

When I worked on a storage system at IBM, we were in an area of the organization that was very remote from the actual users. In all truth, we hardly understood parts of the system itself. There was a concept in the system that we had to write code around and allow customers to manage—without ever really grasping what it meant. It was as if we were hearing a language we didn't speak and were just attempting to utter the exact words back.

This lack of understanding, of course, had tangibly affected our productivity. A lot of rework was needed when we misunderstood how things operated. All of that could have been spared had we been taught what all of these words meant. To this day, it remains a running gag among our old team. Today, I prefer to see teams find other ways to be "funny."

Rubbing Elbows

Providing product mastery means that the tech people should understand business initiatives better and, therefore, be more attuned to customers' needs. A similar, yet different, area worth exposing to them is how others in the company work. When other professions are treated as "black boxes," there is no dialog going on. Whatever requests or information we receive are taken at face value. Just as product mastery makes the customers "real" in our minds, working together with others in the company enables more impactful collaboration.

If we reduce friction by ensuring each department is ensconced and doesn't "bother" others, we lose out on this. Putting in place elaborate processes and procedures intended to prevent human interactions might be well intended but ill destined nevertheless. In case the organization is suffering from the existing communication, the solution is to find the root causes and fix them, not avoid contact altogether. Otherwise, we end up not just creating silos but fortifying them.

On the contrary, when we have healthy friction going on, we make the work of everyone visible. That allows the product and engineering teams to understand it better and gain insights. Those, in turn, might be used to improve the product or for investment in internal operations. An example of the former would be the teams that start percolating possible improvements after witnessing firsthand what customers were going through when they stay with Customer Success, as mentioned in Chapter 1.

The latter case, where teams decide to invest in internal improvements, is no less interesting. Learning of internal workflows, bottlenecks, and opportunities might trigger efforts to leverage technology internally. The companies that leverage technology the best have a mindset of **Coders Without Borders**. Tech investment is not limited solely to feature development, and might be used for creating internal infrastructure and work tools, whenever that makes business sense.

Chapter 6, which covers innovation and tech capital, touches more on this subject. For now, suffice to say that intermissions or hackathons where internal facing improvements are made can be invaluable and more impactful than many sprints of feature development. You have to be willing to allocate your tech efforts to what would move the needle, even if it seems odd to work on internal tools initially. This way, R&D can create force multipliers that give others in the company little superpowers that make them more effective and help accelerate the company's momentum on all fronts.

NO-CODE TO ELIMINATE MONOPOLIES

Another aspect of creating "cyborgs" and unlocking total tech leverage is ensuring enough freedom to use it. The "problem" is that sometimes when others in the company come up with their own ideas about how technology might be helpful for them, they have to "sell" this idea to product and engineering so it would get prioritized. It is not genuinely a problem because that is the healthy route for new requests. They have to be weighed against everything else and be put on the roadmap solely if that makes sense.

However, this efficiency is not ideal for those who now feel at a loss. They have reached the point we want—they can vividly imagine and discern where technology might be helpful for them. All that, and now their needs aren't prioritized? This situation sometimes makes others in the company call R&D a "monopoly," being the sole providers of technology within the company. That does not have to be the case.

Every day more tools are being created that enable mere mortals to do what was previously only possible for coders. These are called no-code/low-code tools. By being laser-focused on specific use cases and assumptions, they can sometimes replace weeks of coding work with a few clicks of the mouse. While still relatively new, more and more companies are adding such services to their toolset and gaining incredible results.

For example, many have gotten used to connecting different services together using Zappier instead of having to go through code-based integrations and handling custom APIs. Virtually anyone can shave a few tedious minutes off their days with a personal automation on IFTTT (or even just set it up to let you know in the morning that it is going to rain, and you better grab an umbrella). I've seen marketing and content people create complex email campaigns single-handedly using ConvertKit that would otherwise require weeks of development.

Creating Autonomy, Not Anarchy

Just as described earlier regarding the integration of stand-alone tools, just because no-code tools are easy to add doesn't mean they should be added haphazardly. Most of these require permissions to be given to them and might access sensitive data. They are also easy to get out of hand and be hard to maintain. Instead of creating a menagerie of tools, try to pinpoint a couple to start with that can serve many important needs. Then, slowly add more.

IT needs to be involved to ensure that there are no cyber risks involved or potential problems on existing systems, but this involvement should be kept to a minimum. The whole point of using these tools is to allow others in the company to be independent and tinker on their own.

Not a Silver Bullet

I can already sense that some of you are wondering why can't these tools be used to replace your engineers. Well, as we say to the god of death: not today. While no-code tools can replace certain aspects of your product, what currently exists cannot replace all of them. Eventually, the team comes upon a particular customization need requiring handcrafted solutions. Furthermore, these tools will never be as flexible or performant as bespoke code can be. That is why many companies use these tools in the initial stages to move quickly. If and when the value has been established, and volume grows, these parts are then replaced by the R&D team.

Nevertheless, no-code is extremely useful for parts of the system that are not customer-facing—for example, creating internal tools that make people's lives a bit easier. I would also say that these should be used by R&D regularly. Those more technical should also look at low-code tools. These are similar to no-code offerings but allow for more customizations using minimal coding logic where appropriate. As part of your focus on delivering value rapidly and validating ideas, using such tools for prototypes and beta versions can feel magical.

ACTION ITEMS

By now, you should have identified at least a couple of areas where your company's culture could use some improvement. Since many of the mindset and work changes take time, I recommend picking a couple to start with.

- Ask your tech executives to create a tech orientation workshop for the senior leadership team.
- In your next offsite, save a portion of the time to consider different tools and options. Perhaps even tinker with a few. This should result in a packed list of worthy initiatives.
- Ensure that your regular onboarding and periodical training cover the needed tech aspects.
- Spot good candidates in your existing processes for injecting more healthy friction.

NOTES

1. Objectives and Key Results, a goal-setting framework popularized by Andy Grove, Intel's founder. https://en.wikipedia.org/wiki/OKR.
2. See https://gong.io.
3. See https://www.descript.com.
4. See https://gloat.com.
5. For more resources about gaining product mastery from the R&D side, see the extra resources mentioned in the Conclusion.

5

In-House, Outsource, Build vs. Buy?: Your Technology Force Structure

An obvious advantage is that software, as opposed to hardware, is innately more malleable and flexible. That strong point is too often diluted because, as flexible as software can be, it also abides by Conway's law. Therefore, whatever organizational structure you decide to use significantly impacts the team's effectiveness, and these structures are orders of magnitude harder to change. After all, employees don't thrive in environments that go through quarterly reorganizations or changing managers and teams capriciously.

A considerable portion of the effort to leverage your tech talent is about your tech force structure, composition, and size. It is also often a contention point between senior leadership and the other tech executives. This chapter aims to supply you with the tools to engage in these arguments intelligently and equipped with models to make the right decisions.

TECH IN THE ORG CHART

The first problem to tackle before we go into the composition of your tech team is where it should be located within the organizational structure. In all honesty, there are several options and plenty of evidence supporting and disputing each option. There is no one absolute truth. Nevertheless, everything else being equal, there are options that, in my experience, are easier to execute.

DOI: 10.4324/9781003358473-5

Your Tech Leadership Chain-of-Command

In Chapter 2, we already saw the importance of tech executives for any tech initiative to succeed. Nevertheless, merely deciding to have these leaders is not enough. The organizational structure affects the types of relationships and initiatives you will see.

Get Your Tech Leaders

First and foremost, I have to stress how utterly critical it is to have real tech leaders as part of your organization. By that, I mean that whoever you select to lead the initiative should be an employee of your company and full-time on it. Anything else is not appropriate for any serious tech initiative.

It is becoming increasingly common today to use the services of external experts for these responsibilities. You might have encountered people with offerings like CTO-as-a-Service or Fractional VP Engineering. Essentially, these are professionals who spend their time working with multiple companies concurrently and take on these responsibilities for them. I have no axe to grind with these offerings. I used to do it myself and might still be asked to help an existing client during a crisis or in case of a leadership gap.

However, I never kid myself or my clients that this is a viable situation in the long term. While not entirely the same, I'm going to assume you wouldn't want a "fractional CEO" heading your company. Tech leaders are most effective when they are able to invest all of their cognitive energy in one company. The focus allows them to come up with better plans, be immersed in your company's needs, and have a genuine mastery of your product. This is simply impossible when juggling a few clients.

For companies that are very small and just starting out, with a tech staff of a couple of people, using these fractional offerings can be helpful for the first few months. Even then, it would be better to have the leadership talent in-house. Whatever happens, I find that having such situations last more than six months is unhealthy.

Tech Leadership Reporting to Whom?

Tech leadership has to be given enough access and credit to affect the company's strategy and roadmap. Therefore, whether you have C-level or VP-level leaders, they should report directly to one of the most senior people in the company. For many, that would be the CEO or the COO. In some companies, there are both a CTO and a VP in charge of the R&D group. In those cases, I would default to the VP reporting to whoever the CTO reports to, but that is not set in stone.

To help you, assess which of you is most appropriate and capable of this. Sometimes, when the CEO and COO are much in sync, there is no real difference, and it merely comes down to the COO being more available or having more context. However, let us use a hypothetical company where the COO is involved in the matters of the current quarter while the CEO comes up with strategic goals that might span years. A tech executive that solely communicates with the COO can ensure alignment with the company's current plans but will miss out on the opportunity to see what's coming ahead, prepare the team accordingly, and inject innovation into the roadmap. That means that even then, effective tech executives will do their best to maintain an ongoing relationship with the CEO and other executives.

Another aspect of this decision is who tech's counterparts are reporting to. When your teams are cross-functional, as we will cover later in this chapter, a tight relationship among the different leaders is needed. Therefore, strive for an organizational structure that places these leaders as peers.

A particular instance of this question is whether your R&D and Product leads should report to an executive that effectively "compartmentalizes" product engineering, as shown in Figure 5.1. There are effectively two options that are common today.

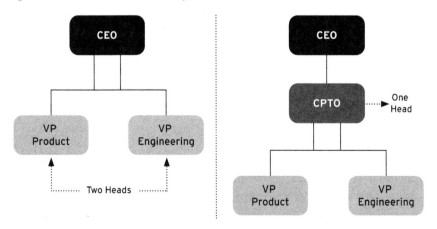

FIGURE 5.1
Two heads vs. one-head structure.

Two heads: Product and R&D executives might report to the CEO or the COO, along with a whole cadre of executives in this scenario. This approach is effective when the company doesn't have a technical cofounder and when we want to promote collaboration between these leaders and the rest of the executive team. Of course, it requires that who they report to can "referee" when arguments inevitably occur.

One head: Compartmentalizing product engineering under the wing of a single executive, for example, a CPTO,[1] can circumvent certain issues. First, if both tech and engineering leaders are not as senior or lack enough product mastery, having a single "face" for product engineering can make leading tech initiatives and digital transformations easier. Second, if the two leaders have different gravitas within the company, it might create an imbalance where one side steamrolls the other. Such a structure can ensure a healthier equilibrium and that both sides are heard. Having a leader that can effectively manage both of these is not common. I tend to say that if you have someone capable of it, you probably know it. In that case, there is no harm in doing so.

Effective Organizational Structure

In each company, there are those departments that tend to grow, sometimes rapidly, and those that stay relatively the same. For most tech-driven companies, the R&D team does not remain static for too long. Due to that, and to engineers having a proclivity to organize things, these departments have hierarchy introduced sooner than others. Agreeing on a healthy structure will ensure that your R&D organization can grow with time with the least amount of reorganizations and interruptions.

Too Many Cooks

As a rule of thumb, R&D teams generally do well, with around six individual contributors per team. That number can be lower for new teams or go as high as a dozen for teams with very senior staff and an experienced manager. Six members mean that the manager should have enough "airtime" with each one for ongoing coaching and mentoring while also not drowning in having to synchronize everything.

Continuing with this logic, one manager-of-managers—often styled as a Director of Engineering—should manage about six such managers. Thus, you have seven managers in charge of thirty-six engineers. That ends up with a managerial overhead of 1:6, which is pretty good so that no manager is understaffed or overworked. I've seen companies make mistakes that start them on a very silly path early on.

I once saw an early-stage company that, for myriad reasons, ended up with a hierarchy so ridiculous that they had more full-time managers than full-time software engineers. The overhead meant that every detail that had to be communicated had to go through too many people. The result reminded me of children playing "telephone." In addition, the precedent they set made others anticipate similar promotions. All in all, it resulted in a significant waste of time, effort, and managerial trust at a formative stage. Undoing that required months and with some talent lost.

While this was an extreme case, these sorts of issues are precisely what will happen if you let politics and weird structures rear their heads. While tech folks are great at spotting tech debt—areas in the code that require upkeep and maintenance—they tend to be more oblivious regarding organizational debt. Sometimes, it is up to senior leadership to help set the tone.

Don't Overdo the Supportive Roles

While too many managers might be easier to spot, one should also be aware of the senior tech staff and their effectiveness. R&D teams frequently have the more senior engineers take roles such as "tech lead" or "software architect." These supportive roles usually don't have managerial responsibility and can act as genuine force multipliers in organizations.

However, these, like managers, should be kept at a sane ratio to the rest of the team. Furthermore, be wary if these roles' responsibilities seem to disengage from any hands-on work. That is a pitfall that steers teams more toward "tech for tech's sake" and effectively increases the managerial overhead in your company.

Cross-Functional Teams

Aligning teams for maximal impact requires ensuring collaboration across disciplines. One way for senior leadership to enforce this is to put in place business objectives that are shared across departments. If you use these, you will regularly hear your tech executives clamor for cross-functional teams. That's a good sign!

Cross-functional teams are task forces that cooperate in order to achieve an objective. The first level of "cross-functional" is where engineering teams are divided not by technological areas but by business ones. This way, you don't have backend, frontend, iOS, and Android teams. Instead, there are teams around specific areas of your product, each containing whatever talent is needed to move forward fast.

Taking cross-functional concepts up a notch, it is excellent to form teams that are more than merely a cadre of engineers. Those are teams with product managers, UI designers, marketing people, and so on. Essentially, they include whoever is required to get the work done end-to-end. In these scenarios, people do not usually report to managers from other departments but do work closely together on large-scale objectives. This is one of the areas where senior leadership has a tangible impact on how effective their teams can be.

While it is more common for R&D and Product leaders to want to work in these teams, there are still objections from the other departments. Sales and marketing people who never worked in such structures might find it strange or uncomfortable at first. Your tech executives cannot enforce such a structure out of their teams. It is up to you to enable it and support their initiatives.

IN-HOUSE AND OUTSOURCE

While tech executives shouldn't be outsourced, it is commonplace to have teams composed of a mix of in-house employees and outsourced contractors. Deciding on the suitable composition for your scenario requires weighing company needs and constraints, as well as the preference of your tech leaders. Here are the things that you should keep in mind.

Company Constraints

First, the different constraints have to be communicated to the tech executives so that they can come up with the optimal structure. Too often, these are not realized before it is too late. Therefore, you should review these with your executive team and provide guidance.

Budget: There is no beating around the bush. Knowing which options are relevant relies heavily on how much you are able to invest into R&D. Openly discuss the possible ranges of budgets, both currently and the expected growth through the course of the next 18–24 months. Given that engineers' pay seems to be doing better than the stock market, you should consider that even maintaining a static team often requires the budget to get bigger with time.

Regulation: I have worked with companies where decisions such as in-house vs. outsourcing were straightforward because of regulatory needs or considerations. For example, some government contracts might require that the staff be local and/or citizens. Another consideration is the different employment laws that should be heeded. Many European Union startups start by hiring staff as contractors due to it being easier to let go of someone who turns out to be a bad match.

Culture: Some companies, as a principle, refrain from relying on outsourcing companies or contractors. While personally, I do not think this is the right call (but I am biased, having worked as one for years and seeing it succeed), it is a legitimate company policy that affects your organizational structure.

Business Needs: Mostly top of mind for public companies but also relevant for those seeking investment, the structure of your spending can also be relevant to how you shape R&D. A tech force comprising employees will be categorized as Capital Expenditure. On the other hand, using contractors or a tech agency goes on the books as Operational Expenditure (CapEx and OpEx, respectively). Thus, some companies might have value in showing that they have grown their tech talent in-house or reducing their CapEx by relying mainly on contractors.

Team Composition Patterns

Other than company constraints, the other side of team composition is about the preference of your tech leaders. As they will be accountable for the team's performance, they should get a say about its structure and who to put on it. Since the different work modes might seem a bit odd to those not used to it, let us quickly go over the most frequent team composition patterns that are not entirely in-house. This will allow you to assess whether your tech executives are making decisions that conform to the company's stage and culture.

The Proof-of-Concept Team: Whether for a brand new group being formed or as part of a new and disconnected initiative, it is often necessary to hit the ground running fast. At the proof-of-concept (POC) stage, your tech leaders might have questions about the right technology and the type of employees they will need. This is a typical case for relying on a software agency for the initial kickoff. Outsourced engineers working in tandem with your tech leaders start the work on the project.

As the risks are addressed, and the fog of war starts to clear these often gradually become less reliant on the external vendor. Depending on your needs, this might be in the form of slowly hiring a team and disengaging the vendor or moving into a staff augmentation arrangement.

THE NEVER-ENDING REWRITE

This is the story of one company but also the story of too many companies. The CEO of a startup that had a product out approached me. They were getting market traction and had displayed that their idea works with tens of thousands of users. Nevertheless, the tech side was underperforming.

The company did not have a tech executive or team but relied on an outsourcing agency to do all the work. Therefore he couldn't assess how well they were working, and the agency failed to connect to the business and its future needs. Cut to six months later, and that agency said the product would have to be rewritten to support the company's needs.

He replaced the agency, and another came in and performed that rewrite. Unfortunately, the same thing happened within less than a year. Only later, when a tech executive was put in place and ensured that all tech efforts were aligned with the company's needs, did they manage to get a sustainable product that didn't perform like a disposable prototype.

Skunkworks: Innovation is one of the most impactful things an R&D team can spend time on. Unfortunately, it is also regularly cast aside while companies focus on short-term needs. For this reason, CTOs sometimes put up teams that focus on innovative projects and being on the lookout for "the next big thing." These might be called the CTO Office, Skunkworks, Innovation teams, Labs, etc. Because these teams often require highly skilled engineers and flexibility, they can frequently be staffed with expert contractors and consultants. That also has the benefit of quickly getting started.

Experts: Given the rapid pace of technology, you can expect to require something the team does not currently know how to do. When these situations arise, you don't always have to go for a POC mode with an external team. Sometimes, it is sufficient to bring in a couple of experts, even part-time, who provide guidance and help the planning process. These consultants can save considerable time and effort by sharing their experience.

A typical example is when companies that already have a website decide that they would also like to have a mobile application. It is likely that none of the current team members are experts in this realm, so contracting an expert can allow the team to get to work faster while the engineers learn the ropes of mobile development.

Staff Augmentation: Especially given the challenging landscape of hiring in tech, relying on contractors and agencies to get more people on the team fast can be valuable. Staff augmentation often means that these external employees are spread in the entire organization and take on work in groups like anyone else. While they are quicker to onboard, they also tend to have a higher turnover than company employees. This has to be considered when planning for the organization's robustness.

For example, be aware that critical knowledge should be regularly shared across the entire team to reduce work interference risks if someone moves projects or quits. This is how you increase your bus factor. Nevertheless, staff augmentation can be highly effective. My experience shows that it works best when the contractors are treated as other employees. For example, provide them with the same holiday gifts and invest time in coaching and mentoring them. To paraphrase the old saying, you might find it odd to invest in them since they might leave. However, consider what happens when you don't invest in them, and they *stay*.

Different Teams: Lastly, there is always the possibility of using software agencies to staff entire teams. Ostensibly, this is a simpler model: the external team might already be used to working together. It might be easier if there is a language barrier between one of the team members or when they are in a different time zone (often the case when outsourcing to other countries).

Nevertheless, for the same reasons we've outlined throughout the book so far, experience shows these frequently create small silos disconnected from your business and product and must be managed very carefully. Rather than have a team of autonomous engineers with agency and innovation, you effectively have a bunch of talented people who operate in order-taking mode. It might be better than nothing if you have no other options, but it is definitely not the most effective way of using external help.

WHERE ARE THEY ALL AT? REMOTE AND HYBRID

While the tech industry was always more open to working from home compared to others, there is no denying that the COVID pandemic changed the meaning of an office for R&D teams. Teams that are colocated all the time are no longer the default.

The options aren't binary—in the office or remote. In fact, there is a whole plane of options to pick from. You can dial up or down the "remoteness" of the team. For example, do people come to the office regularly and so have to be in the same area? Do they meet only if they want to, and therefore some might be completely remote and in other countries? Maybe you don't even have an office? Since these have implications for different parts of the company, you should be aware of the considerations and options.

Easiest: Colocated Teams

Teams that all work together in the same office are straightforward when it comes to managing them. When starting up, it lowered communication overhead, and the gains it has for collaboration make it a no-brainer. However, for any sizable organization, it is not always as clear-cut. First, the market has shifted, like it or not. Today's top tech talent is not guaranteed to accept an offer which means they have to commute to the office five days a week—even when that office is within walking distance. Due to these market forces, even if you are inclined to be colocated, you have to ensure it is worth it.

One part is to assess your environment to determine its viability for staying colocated. If you happen to be already headquartered in an area that is a tech talent hub, you have an advantage. Cities that do not attract or grow talent regularly suffer from slimmer pickings, meaning that you will be considerably limiting your company. After all, what are the odds that the handful of available engineers in your town all turn out to be highly productive? Similarly, it is essential to consider how close your team would be to its customers on a grander scale. A company in London building its offering mainly for clients in North America will find it harder to have the engineers engaged with the product if they all live in London.

Second, consider your long-term needs as well as your existing assets. As the laws of supply and demand dictate, if you decide to limit your talent search to your close vicinity, you will have to fight harder for those people. Therefore, be prepared to provide higher compensation and more perks and ensure your war chest will suffice.

Also, what sort of growth trajectory are you aiming for? A business that grows organically does not have the same staffing needs as a scale-up company going through hyper-growth for a few years. If you will need hundreds of engineers, staying confined to one city will be almost impossible unless it is one of the world's leading tech hubs.

Hybrid: Collaboration in Hard-Mode

While a lot more popular than remote-only, hybrid is considerably more challenging. That is due to the fact that you're neither here nor there. For example, depending on how often people arrive at the office, you might have to get office space accommodating the entire team, even though your offices might rarely be at more than 50% capacity.

Furthermore, unless you are able to achieve a delicate balance between those working from home and those at the office, all your meetings, and other communication patterns have to straddle both worlds. Each conference room ought to have suitable equipment to allow people to call in. Every meeting invite has to have a video-call link set up for it. Otherwise, if those working from home have to request these specifically for meetings they want to attend, they will feel like second-class citizens in the company. And they would be right.

Even more challenging is the fact that managing a hybrid workforce requires very mindful and active attention from your managers. Often, they have to acquire new skills. Gone are the days when they can easily count hours in the office as a (rather useless) measure of performance. While this is clearly also the case for fully remote work, it is much more challenging when part of the team is "normal" (from the point of view of those who are used to colocated teams). You have to ensure that your company is not biased against those who choose to work remotely or only get to the office part of the time.

Why, then, is this the most common option today? It has genuine advantages. First, it covers all bases. No one feels left out. Whatever best suits an employee can be provided. It is also somewhat of a necessity for certain teams. For example, if you have several offices that collaborate, the work will be partly hybrid, no matter what. You might as well use that to get better talent and improve your position as an employer. This flexibility can be highly attractive in a world where the fight for top talent is ever-present.

Remote-Only: New-World Collaboration

The mere thought of teams collaborating solely remote for years, without regularly meeting in person, can make many an executive shudder. Even those that were fine when COVID forced them to abandon their office might still find it hard to believe that such a model can be sustainable. In fact, we have plenty of proof that it is an excellent way to create highly valuable and innovative software: open-source. The internet is essentially running on operating systems and frameworks that were written by people that we never met. In many cases, these are not even people that did this as part of their full-time job.

Today, remote-only companies are certainly more popular than they used to be before 2020 but are still the least common collaboration pattern. It creates a company culture that is different from any other and has to fit your vision for the company. The benefits are significant: no office space, genuine flexibility, and a naturally more inclusive culture. It is also possible to have only parts of your organization be remote, such as the R&D and Product teams while keeping sales and marketing teams in your headquarters.

However, execution requires mindful staffing and practices. For example, most remote-only companies aim to have people meet their teammates in person a few times a year and have a company-wide retreat once or twice a year as well. Remote is aimed at organizations with a higher concentration of senior staff than others since the increased autonomy makes it harder for less experienced employees. It also only works well if the company decides to have a genuine culture of articulation. You know the saying, "this meeting could have been an email?" That is doubly more important to avoid in remote, given that remote conferencing seems to fatigue people faster.

The Salad

Some companies find success by defining "pockets" of remote work. Once your organization is sufficiently large, you can have groups that are colocated and others that are hybrid or completely remote. This is different from merely choosing hybrid work because it offers all styles. The collocated team mainly works collocated, while the remote team doesn't have half a group that meets together in an office.

Thus, you can offer something that works for most everyone. I have seen people who swore by remote-only work at a certain stage in their lives but a couple of years later wanted to be back in the office and vice versa. If you stick to the six-person-teams rule of thumb, this sort of setup can be utilized even with less than 20 people.

HOW BIG IS BIG ENOUGH?

The size of your tech team should not be decided without due planning. Merely throwing more people and money at a tough problem might not be enough to solve it or even aggravate it. In other cases, a particular investment threshold is needed to unlock the upper echelons of innovation. Your budget affects what the team can deliver. Those estimations can then cause the budget to change once more. Thus, the budget is more flexible in businesses that are not going through belt-tightening but are actively growing. Maximizing the return on investment relies on effectively communicating all sides' needs, constraints, and abilities.

The Case for Smaller Teams

In a world with ever-increasing team sizes, I always feel the urge to remind business owners that headcount is not everything. We've all seen countless examples of small teams beating big giants in execution. Two very high-profile examples are WhatsApp and Instagram. When Meta acquired them, the former had hundreds of millions of users and the last tens of millions. Surprisingly, both had a dozen or fewer engineers.

Today, many startups with a handful of clients have bigger teams. Mind you, Instagram and WhatsApp were acquired in an era when we didn't have quite as much available to engineers on public clouds and scaling architecture. And they had several different apps, all being developed simultaneously. It's mind-boggling, yet I do not believe those teams were *that* special. They merely had the smarts to focus on specific goals and drive toward them mercilessly.

This is to say that you should keep this in mind when coming up with the budget and plans for your tech team. Do not kid yourself that every team can be as highly effective, but be certain: your team can surely be *more* effective with the proper constraints. If you keep increasing your headcount it has to be because you can see the gains. Do not keep throwing more engineers at something that doesn't work.

Rules of Thumb for Team Sizes

Anything less than two full-time engineers can hardly be referred to as a team. A team of two individual contributors and a manager is an atom for any reliable product delivery. Any less than that, and your projects become highly prone to delays in cases of vacations or sick leave. Usually, such small teams have engineers considered "full stack," meaning they can cover all areas of technology needed for product delivery.

Generally, attempt to keep the related tech force to about a handful of team members until the initiative has proven its viability (the so-called Product-Market Fit). Of course, one might have several such teams working on different projects simultaneously.

For bigger projects with a broader scope, the team size for each product can increase accordingly. One aspect that requires bigger teams is when there is a need for specific specialties. Today, such specialties include AI or machine learning knowledge and expertise in specific technical areas such as hardware integration, novel algorithms, cryptography, and cyber research.

Every area of technology that is still relatively new often requires such expertise, but as time goes on, the barrier to entry lowers, and your full-stack engineers might be able to do most of the work. Some time ago, it was common to have teams of backend, frontend, and mobile engineers all separate, the latter often even split to different platforms, iOS, and Android. With the advancement of tools, I have seen plenty of talented senior engineers that can do all these by themselves, even though they might not be considered experts. Each full-stack engineer often brings flexibility like a wildcard, while specialists are too often set in stone. If you realize that direction is not needed a few months later or that most of the work has been done there, they cannot be easily moved to a different project.

Software teams do not scale linearly quickly, which means that you cannot simply decide to add more people to a late project and hope that it will be done faster. Further, a "too many cooks" scenario is possible when several people are tasked with working on overlapping areas of the code. Those usually have a high overhead of communication and synchronization and should be avoided.

Beyond that, it is hard to tell exactly how many people are needed for each organization, as circumstances, needs, and abilities have a tremendous effect. I would say that roughly 75% of significant features (e.g., not minor tweaks or monumental overhauls) should be done by 2–3 people within 2–6 weeks. Some capable engineers would tend toward the bottom of that range, while others would require more time. Thus, after seeing the average performance of the team, you can guesstimate what it will be able to achieve with time and whether more staffing is needed.

One last bit of advice is not to get used to a certain speed. If your engineering team has been producing similar types of features regularly, they should be getting better at it. It is novel work that should take more time. I know this goes against common beliefs, which assume that organizations become slower with time. I beg to differ. The best teams hone how similar work is done so that it becomes easier with time.

Build vs. Buy

As part of shaping your team and budget, be aware that there are often more possibilities than merely creating a custom solution using X or Y engineers, in-house or outsourced. One might prefer to rely on existing products and services rather than hand-code them. This "build vs. buy" sort of decision is very common in all sizes of projects.

In fact, any engineering team regularly makes use of external tools. They host their servers on cloud providers, which also offer various platforms and tools. They rely on open-source frameworks for day-to-day work. SaaS solutions can be regularly used to solve problems, big or small. However, when these external services aren't free, like open-source frameworks, but require payment, some companies make the wrong trade-off.

It is straightforward to externally look at expenses such as cloud costs and request that the team "tighten its belt." While such housekeeping is needed from time to time, generally, I believe teams are not using external tools enough. The Not-Invented-Here Syndrome is about engineers who prefer to write too many things themselves, believing that the tailored solution is the right one. That should be the case for work that is core to your business and your edge in the market. Peripheral tech needs can be fulfilled with external tools whenever possible.

After all, even if you save some monthly expenses, you have to consider the (high) cost of engineers investing their time to fix it. You might hear someone say, "we can replace that product with one engineer!" Yes, that might be possible, to an extent. But do not underestimate what a whole other business is doing. Also, do not forget that a single engineer is bound to take time off, sick leave, or even leave the company. That is not a problem when you rely on an external service.

Default to use what the world has to offer. When something becomes so big that economies of scale apply and it makes sense to replace it with a custom solution, do it. Do not rush for premature optimization of the cost before necessary.

The Right Investment

Team size is also dependent on your intentions. The above advice should suffice if you have a product idea that you would like your product engineering team to deliver. However, for those who genuinely aim to disrupt, innovate, and create technology that is the best in the world? They will have to invest considerably more.

Many Fortune 100 companies spend a considerable part of their budget on R&D. That is because real innovation requires placing bets, trying things, and seeing what happens. More on that in the next chapter. For now, I will just stress the importance of realizing what your intentions are as part of sizing your team correctly.

ACTION ITEMS

Whether you are currently setting up your tech team or planning your budget for the next couple of years, start with this:

- Be clear about your intentions and the type of organization you are looking to create.
- Choose (or shift to) an organizational structure that doesn't introduce unnecessary overhead.
- Assess which of the current projects on your roadmap might benefit from one of the outsourcing patterns described.
- Set a goal for your team's size and composition and start working toward it.

NOTE

1. See Chapter 2.

6

Habitual Innovation and Tech Capital: Creating Offensive Creativity On-Demand

Semantic satiation is what happens when you hear or read the same word so much it seems to no longer make sense. "Innovation" is a word that suffers from it regularly. It gets thrown around so much today that the connection between what teams actually do and genuine innovation is often slim to nonexistent. In all seriousness, I've seen a company boasting on its social media about the "innovative" change of color palette on its website.

R&D teams are a major part of most companies' budgets precisely because they have the ability to provide a lot of novelty and value that can materially improve the business. However, executives often claim to have an environment that fosters creativity yet drive their people to always focus on immediate results. When we are too myopic, we will never notice opportunities to innovate, even if they are right in front of us.

THE CURRENT STATE OF INNOVATION

Creativity usually comes in two meager forms for companies that are not consciously working on cultivating innovation. The first is the *innovation facade*, similar to the color change mentioned above.

While that example might seem obviously nonsensical, similar, yet craftier, manifestations are everywhere. Every enterprise application you have used in the past that patted itself on the back for adding an ability

DOI: 10.4324/9781003358473-6

that had become standard a few years earlier is a testimony of the slow adaptation of even off-the-shelf innovation—those ideas that were new but easily replicable.

As a matter of setting higher standards, never celebrate that the team has "finally" done something trivial. I am all about celebrating wins, but this is more akin to celebrating remembering to get to the game on time, not winning it. Innovation should be timely and, well, innovative. An easy test is to think about whether it sparks any sense of wonder, surprise, or excitement.

The other typical pattern of low innovation is the *innovation starvation*. Why starvation? Because organizations set up frameworks that are intended to facilitate innovation but end up educating the staff that innovation is something that happens rarely. If that sounds weird, consider the commonplace practice of holding hackathons once or twice a year. The vast majority of companies that do these have a similar pattern: a couple of days of "innovative" work that is not necessarily related to the current roadmap. These bursts of innovation rarely happen more than once every six months.

Hackathons suffer from a few significant drawbacks. First, they confine creativity to a couple of days a year. Effectively, everyone on your team gets the message that creativity is reserved for these few precious days. The rest of the year, they are supposed to zip it and plow ahead. Thus the hackathons—which are supposed to encourage creativity—achieve the opposite and imbue a compartmentalizing mindset on the team.

Second, hackathons that are just a couple of days are too short to delve into anything of significance. Such a short time frame is barely enough for some basic proofs of concept, especially when the area is one the team is inexperienced at. The time crunch also means that those engineers on the team who are driven to show something at the end of the hackathon tend to take fewer risks precisely when we want them to feel freer and bolder.

Moreover, too often, these hackathons have no tangible results beyond a couple of lovely photos for the company's social media. Frequently, teams finish them with about half of the initiatives yet unfinished. Mind you that is not a 50% success rate for taking risks. It is merely an issue of not having enough time, or failing to reduce scope sufficiently, and therefore not seeing the experiment through. No one even knows if it is worth it or not at the end of the hackathon. Other times, the created tools and innovations have a tendency to be too developer-oriented. While such improvements clearly have their place, they should not constitute the majority of the work.

With the proper guidance and leeway, your team can do much better. Wouldn't it be nice if, at the end of these pushes for innovation, the team had things so exciting to show that it would feel like an internal version of an Apple event? The magic of Apple events is that while supply chain leaks often tell us a lot about the hardware ahead of time, we rarely have any intelligence about the software changes. Therefore, every time we are surprised to see how they push through current boundaries. Your developers can achieve the equivalent internally.

TYPES OF INNOVATION

What should you be aiming for? Creativity can push you forward in many directions. A healthy team ensures to maintain a healthy balance of all these.

Incremental improvements: These are often smaller scale changes that are not groundbreaking but steadily push the company forward. Examples include finding ways to optimize some product processes or reduce costs slightly. This sort of innovation will rarely take the company to new places or unlock remarkable capabilities. Often this is the type of thing we see in hackathons: someone had an idea about doing something slightly better, and they made that happen.

Leap up: More than an incremental improvement, a leap up happens when there is a substantial upgrade to how things are currently done. You might have heard the saying, "work smarter, not harder." This is what a leap up often means. Therefore, it is not about introducing new capabilities but about making existing features demonstrably better. That alone, though, can change how things are done and provide a lot more value to users. For example, engineers might change an existing feature so that it can be run much quicker. Therefore, your users can preview changes immediately as opposed to only after they actively save their changes or allow the company to supply a specific feature as part of its free offering because its marginal cost has decreased significantly.

Sharp turns: A move from the current way of doing things. Sometimes, you shouldn't work harder or smarter, but simply *differently*. Consider smartphone cameras. While makers still eke out better specs for their cameras with every new model, there is a physical limit to how much a lens can be improved within the confines of a small smartphone. That is why some years ago, Apple started investing heavily in enhancing photography using software, like portrait mode, that attempts to mimic the bokeh effect.

Frequently, these sharp turns are not initially part of the product roadmap. That is because they rely on technological changes that are currently foreign to the company, and therefore, not many can even envision them. Once the value is demonstrated, though, the best teams pounce on these opportunities.

Tech capital: Whereas many engineering teams wallow in complaints about the *tech debt* that they are amassing, the best teams generate tech capital. It is different than creating more code and churning out feature requests. Tech capital is about creating technology that makes the organization itself better and faster. Have you ever discovered a keyboard shortcut that has saved you countless hours over the years? Tech capital is the same—for your team.

Figure 6.1 helps demonstrate the differences between these manifestations of creativity.

ARE YOU INNOVATING?

We let ourselves off the hook when it comes to innovation because it seems like it should happen by itself. After all, it is not merely a matter of blocking an hour on the calendar with the title "be creative." However, there are definitely steps that companies can take to increase their current level of novelty and make it more common. To start, you must be able to tell whether your team is even innovating and how often. Without measuring it somewhat, you won't be able to tell how much attention is needed nor easily spot the improvements.

At the level of the executive team, a summary of changes implemented over the last period should be given. This should be reviewed every two to

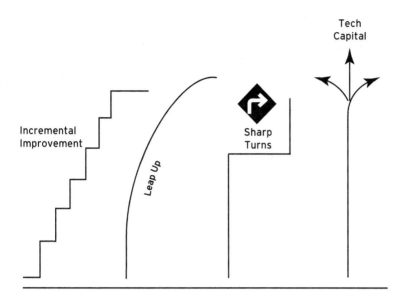

FIGURE 6.1
The different types of innovation.

three months. An innovation review can categorize the accomplishments according to the types defined above.

Measuring Innovation

Many organizations find it difficult to even put their finger on innovative progress that was accomplished. It tends to go unnoticed. First, it is due to the nature of creativity. When innovation is habitual and commonplace, it is more of a natural evolution than a single act. Thus, someone might have had the intuition to try something. That didn't work exactly as expected, but someone else got another idea off of it. Then it was forgotten for a month and eventually repurposed as a feature developed by the team. Much like Theseus's ship that had all its parts replaced by the time it was back to port, it might no longer be easy to discern the spark was an engineer's inkling.

Second, sometimes it doesn't even feel like any creativity is involved, but merely professionals doing their jobs. Those who stay current with the latest technological changes often do so because they have a passion for it and not because they are looking for valuable applications. Therefore, they do not feel like they have done anything special when they find an idea that saved the team a lot of time.

To help the team keep score of its innovation, they should consider the following aspects whenever they compile an update for a review.

Categorize: Using categories of innovation can help the team become aware of its actions. Categories can be the types of innovation mentioned earlier, but you might also find other categories useful for your team. For example, you might divide it into novelties in different parts of your value chain, business impact, or the most affected department.

The exact categories you choose don't matter too much, and you should not spend hours coming up with the categories that are "just right." Their power is in priming brains to notice them. In my experience, merely having categories is enough to make the team more conscious of its efforts. If team members start debating whether a particular change belongs in one category or another, shut that down quickly.

Another helpful aspect of categories is that you can more easily spot if there is an area that is being neglected. An R&D group that can solely show incremental improvements with no larger impact initiatives should probably learn to think bigger. Aim for a healthy mix.

Unscheduled work: Another trick up my sleeve to help teams uncover their own innovation is to ask them to go over the last few months of work delivered and collect those things that weren't originally on the roadmap. Not all of those are necessarily innovative. For example, perhaps the business development department created an opportunity for a collaboration that had to be done then and there.

However, many innovative ideas do have their roots in unplanned work. Due to their grassroots nature, these changes are often pushed between other tasks. Sometimes this measure is harder to use because the team instinctively tries to hide and minimize awareness of any unplanned work that was done. After all, too much unplanned work is not a good thing. In general, you should avoid shooting messengers even if you discover a lot of unplanned work. Find the root cause for this and treat it disconnected from the innovation metrics.

Count failures: Innovation attempts cannot all be successful. Often, the team will invest time in efforts that don't end up succeeding but were nevertheless worth attempting. While having a quarter composed solely of honest tries that didn't pan out is not what you are aiming for, keeping track of bets placed is worthwhile. The team should count the experiments that failed if, even in hindsight, they think they had solid reasoning to do them.

How Much Innovation Is OK?

The amount of creativity turned into results one should expect to see is very hard to put the finger on. First, what you should be aiming for changes with the company's situation. For example, for companies at an embryonic stage, we often need less sharp turns and more focus and delivery on the current roadmap to validate the business's direction. Second, it also depends on the size of your R&D department and its goals. A dozen people are not likely to produce the same results as a team tenfold the size.

Therefore, I recommend measuring your innovation level as described and tracking its progress. As the product matures and the team grows, you should naturally see more innovation happening. Further, assess the quality of this innovation. What you should measure qualitatively is the impact of the said innovation on the company overall. In today's tech climate, companies that don't reinvent or evolve significant parts of their product every 18 months or so are likely to fall behind.

FOSTERING INNOVATION

I will go ahead and assume that after you have measured your innovation to understand your starting point, you realized that you have room for improvement. This then raises the question of how to do it. How can you boost creativity in your company? One thing that I can guarantee you will not work is plastering the wall with "motivational" messages or scheduling that yearly hackathon.

Certain environments produce better results than others. The work environment can cultivate creativity and increase your team's serendipity, or it can hinder all innovation efforts. The executive team plays a major role in shaping the company's culture around novelty.

Creativity Requires Capacity

First and foremost, senior leadership has to come to terms with how creativity works. You shouldn't treat your engineers as precious snowflakes, but you should also realize how your environment affects their daily work. I've heard of sales executives that asked to see a per-person breakdown of engineer productivity by some objective measure. Unfortunately, engineers cannot be measured as easily as salespeople. You cannot set a monthly lines-of-code quota like you might give a team a sales goal.

A general sense of urgency is healthy. It helps people cut on unnecessary work and strive to complete things so they can move on to the next goal. However, too much urgency brings with it tunnel vision. When constantly rushing from one thing to the next, there is no time to actually *think*. Instead, we default to doing what we already know how to do. Therefore, teams that are constantly blitzing rarely have any real innovation. When they always feel like they are behind schedule, senior engineers are not likely to prioritize tinkering with an idea that might just waste time and end up missing deadlines.

Why do we get our best ideas in the shower? Because we are forced to disconnect from the daily rush of work and finally let our minds wander for a bit. This sort of brain state will not be triggered if the team is rushing. Thus, you should not aim to have a team constantly feeling the stress of looming deadlines to a level that creates this atmosphere. You should also refrain from micromanaging and keeping them on a tight leash. There is a fine line between a sense of urgency and anxiety. Do not aim to have every single objective be a stretch goal.

Introduce Intermissions

The wiggle room created in the previous step should make the team more aware of innovation opportunities and help get their creative juices flowing. However, acting on those ideas still requires more time than one might find between quotidian tasks. While this is what some companies use hackathons for, my tried and tested suggestion is to consider **intermissions** instead.

Intermissions sometimes go by different names, such as innovation weeks or sabbaticals. Essentially, these are longer stretches of time where the team works together on other innovative ideas. One major difference is that intermissions are often a full workweek instead of the commonplace two-day hackathon (half of which tends to be spent on company celebrations and demoes). Investing in such a week about once a quarter is often incredibly impactful.

By allocating this amount of time to innovation, many teams find that their productivity is improved during the rest of the time. While counterintuitive initially, this makes sense considering the cost of context switching and cognitive loads. When talented engineers have an idea and want to act on it without having any official time allocated to it, they might try to make progress on it in little bites. The problem is that these little bites create what is known as "open loops" in their minds which collectively create cognitive load.

On the other hand, when the team knows that an intermission is scheduled (on average, about 5–6 weeks away), they can more easily put the idea aside, trusting they will get ample time to try it out. Thus, while you are on paper reducing the time the team spends on regular feature development, you gain productivity. The whole is larger than the sum of its parts.

Beware, though: intermissions should not be turned into a grab bag of ideas and bugs that the CEO or others in the company want to promote and skip the due process. They should really be centered around high-potential experiments aligned with the company's goals.

Similarly, they should also not become refactoring or tech debt weeks. The objective is that at the end of intermissions, we will have a list of insights and learnings. Some are ideas that didn't work. Others might require a different attempt in the next intermissions. A few will have proven value, and then what follows is in-depth work for putting this newfound capability on the roadmap. When the experiment turns into a new ability used in production, it is deemed a success, and you can register another win.

If you are wondering why you have not heard of these from your tech leadership team, there are a few possible reasons. First, intermissions are not yet as popular as hackathons are. Second, many tech executives are afraid even to suggest such a thing, as it might register as time-wasting or naval gazing. But if you understand how this concept works, you can initiate a discussion about how intermissions would look in your company.[1]

Every single company I've seen implement intermissions stuck with it and reported dramatic results. Intermissions have been implemented in teams of all sizes, and even the most hectic teams benefit from them. CEOs asked after running a few replied with things like "Bonanza," "why haven't we done it earlier," and "we want to expand this outside of R&D." Give it an honest shot.

Prioritize Long-Term Research

As great as intermissions can be, they might not be enough to raise your innovation bar to where it should be. Intermissions often generate tangible results regularly, but there is only so much that a talented team can achieve in a single week. This is especially critical for companies relying on deep tech or making use of less mature technology (meaning cutting-edge and rapidly evolving). When this is the case, your tech team might need to regularly research different approaches and changes in the relevant landscape merely to stay current.

In some situations, tech teams might have full-time researchers responsible for these long-term initiatives, but that is not always the case. Sometimes the work doesn't necessitate full-time or requires expertise that cannot be easily handed off to a different person. What happens then is that team members attempt to divide their attention between their daily tasks and long-term experiments, often without being given an organized way to do this process-wise. That is because, often in our industry, we tend to focus solely on urgent tasks and neglect anything that does not come with immediate rewards.

If you want to generate sharp turns at the right time and not always be the last to the party, your team has to be ready. If your tech executives express the need for such research, welcome it. However, do not write blank checks. I recommend allocating specific people and a set amount of time for these experiments—essentially making these longer intermissions. Innovation often loses when there are no constraints, as we will now cover.

CASE STUDY: FROM PARTISAN TO PROFESSIONAL RESEARCH

A company I was working with had leading-edge artificial intelligence models as part of the core of its product. However, once a basic foundation was created, the company's focus was shifted to the surrounding features. The core AI, a significant part of the product's differentiation, ended up being neglected. As competition was rising, they regularly saw how others would beat them to the punch. The CTO was trying to pull people to try new ideas and run experiments under the radar, but that resulted in stunted progress and others becoming irritated with engineers not doing what they were told.

After we discussed the importance of these research activities for the company's future and market position, the executive team decided to change plans and make time for research sprints. While these could result with no tangible results, given that they were experiments, they had to have calculated bets. The team set out to work in this manner for a quarter as a pilot and reviewed its results at the end of it.

When the pilot concluded, everyone reported an improvement. Those who were part of the de facto research team executed more experiments and changes than previously possible. Their output as part of the delivery teams they belonged to most of the quarter was not affected. Even though they had less time for those tasks on paper, not having to try to sneak research tasks in between quotidian duties meant they had less of a cognitive load and were more effective. This is a typical win-win situation exemplifying the whole being greater than the sum of its parts.

Introduce Constraints

Another myth about creativity is that one must leave brilliant minds alone without interruptions or requests. Research efforts not given any boundaries are good at sampling many different things across the entire spectrum of possibilities. However, they usually are awful when it comes to translating those beginnings into production-ready capabilities. This is not new. When Leonardo da Vinci's patrons gave him absolute freedom, he rarely finished any of his works. Some of his best-known paintings were not deemed done by him.

Contrast that with the Israeli army, which is incredibly scrappy compared to that of the United States, the former coming in at about 2.5% of the latter's budget. And yet, time and time again, I saw how 19-year-olds accomplished things their American counterparts—often PhDs and about a tenfold in headcount—failed to achieve. Therefore, my experience shows that it is not all limitations that stymie innovation, only bad limitations.

Rather than giving your research team carte blanche to do as they please, provide them with guiding constraints. These shouldn't damper their creativity but help focus it on actual impact. First, define your investment ahead of time. As in the story above, decide on the resource allocation, meaning how many people will work on this and how long. If you have no time limits, your time is worthless. Put an end date, even if it is seemingly arbitrary, and you will see people push to find creative ways to be done within that time frame.

Second, do not tolerate research sprints that have absolutely no bearing on the company's direction. For example, when a new type of technology emerges, such as blockchains, it is perfectly reasonable for the team to invest part of its research time into getting acquainted with it to assess possible benefits to the business. However, such experiments should be done only if they cover one of these scenarios.

1. The team can come up with hypothetical use cases for the technology even at a very basic level of understanding. This should be evident even in the early brain-storming stages. If they cannot come up with even a hypothetical use, it might be trendy and flashy but not actually useful.
2. The topic of this experiment is relevant to one of the company's strategic directions. For example, even if we cannot yet come up with a use case, a company that has drones as part of its strategic direction would do well to remain apprised of advancements in that field. So researching a new drone navigating technology is a good thing to do, even if initially it doesn't seem applicable to your product or better than your existing solution.
3. They have enough experiments that fit one of the previous two experiments and want to perform a moonshot experiment or as an exercise for getting out of their comfort zone.

Constraints can help make our minds work even harder. Steve Jobs famously would put seemingly impossible demands on teams that only pushed them to create world-changing devices (though, admittedly, I wouldn't want to be on the team that was told it had to replace the iPhone's plastic screen with a glass one within mere months). When one is given a problem along with the assumption it is possible to solve it, it is viewed differently. Contrast how you are likely to act when provided a chess board and asked which move is best and the same board but with the prompt, "white to move and win." The latter will make you think much harder and find a way to get to that win solely due to being told there is a solution. That is the power of constraints: don't just make any move. Go for a win here!

IMPACT OVER NOVELTY

The last part of making innovation habitual in your company is ensuring it remains focused on driving tangible results. While cool demos and proofs of concept might be nice for your company's engineering blog, it doesn't mean much if those never also translate to business improvements. To ensure that the team does not go into "tech for tech's sake," the right mindset and environment must be in place.

A tech team that innovates purely to feel clever is still in the cost-center mindset. A profit-center (enabled, in this case, by innovation) requires a relentless focus on business value.

Tech Capital

Tech capital is meant to be directly opposite to *tech debt* that too many engineers seem obsessed with. Let us start by explaining what teams mean when they talk about their debt and how it is problematic. Tech debt is often defined as the parts of the codebase that require rework to be brought to current standards. Unhandled debt might make the ongoing work of adding new features slower, be more prone to bugs, and increase maintenance costs. It is referred to as "debt" to convey the analogy that it has to be repaid or it worsens with time.

A professional team ensures that its tech debt does not turn into a crippling problem. Much as you would be negligent in letting your house's electrical system deteriorate to a point where it becomes dangerous before renovating it, so shouldn't tech teams grind to a halt because they never spend time ensuring their code is on par with their needs. However, engineers are often attracted to tackling tech debt more than they ought to. Some companies regularly allocate 20–30% of R&D's time to tech debt. I hate taking care of house maintenance, but it definitely isn't that high! Engineers do not focus on tech debt due to laziness. It is essential to understand their thinking in order to tackle it and help them focus their efforts on business results.

It is easier: For many programmers, sitting down and tackling tech debt is where they feel right at home. It is often entirely internal—the changes are not easily discernible to outsiders, much like rewiring your electric box to make it easier to maintain. Therefore, it means there is less communication with outsiders needed. Product managers, for example, are often out of the loop when it comes to these tasks. These tasks then are squarely within the comfort zone of many. One can crank out tech debt tasks freely and feel like they are making progress. Talking to product people, the marketing department, or (**gasp**) users? That is wholly different.

It makes them feel accomplished and challenged: The motivational pull that drives people to a tech focus was covered in Chapter 1. People want to feel like their work matters and that they are progressing. It is a basic human need. Mihaly Csikszentmihalyi coined the term "Flow" to describe deep and challenging work done with great concentration. When coders talk about being "in the zone," they mean they have achieved flow. For many, flow is easier to achieve when the tasks are very technical and easier to define. A chain reaction then forms: every tech debt task brings with it the feeling of accomplishment and progress, and then the engineer would like to see that happen again.

It is where they have control: Look how long we have taken just to explain what tech debt is as part of a digression to get to *tech capital* (we are getting close, I promise). This language barrier means many never take the time to bridge this gap in their daily work. The engineers then learn that they can pull the "tech debt" card and gain the freedom to do what they feel needs to be done. Again, this is not motivated by slacking off but because they genuinely think this is the most important thing to do. Without having real conversations, though, no one can ensure this. Engineers then leverage the language barrier and natural FUD to push their agendas.

This might sound grim, but I believe it is a strikingly accurate depiction of the work processes in many good companies. It is simply so ingrained in how the industry works that we do not stop to consider whether this makes sense. Pointing your team at innovation and tech capital provides you with a way to tackle this and create a win-win situation.

Tech capital is the opposite of maintenance work. It is also not about producing more product features. Tech capital is about R&D groups investing their time in creating force multipliers for the company. When your tech team works as *coders without borders*, it ends up noticing areas of possible improvement internally. The magical power of software, when focused on others in the company, can provide leaps in productivity.

Tech teams are so used to creating tech capital for their own use they do not notice it. For example, they routinely ensure their tests and different pipelines are faster, so engineers waste less time waiting for things daily. The key is realizing that similar opportunities exist everywhere, not just within the tech department. I once saw salespeople's jaws dropping after an engineer took a day to create a tool that consolidated different datasets with the sales department's CRM. Suddenly, they could prioritize and qualify leads much faster, multiplying their chances of success. No one asked the engineer to do this—in fact, the salespeople couldn't even imagine such a thing was possible. It was this ambiance of partnership and *coders without borders* that enabled him to do it.

By making tech capital a common term within the company, you can help direct your team's mental capacity toward where it matters most. Tech capital is also easier to come up with than product- and business-related innovation, making it a great starting point. Tech debt should, of course, be managed, and areas that clearly affect the team's progress should be prioritized, but a healthy team should talk more about amassing capital and not about its debt payments.

Placing Healthy Bets

Although he was talking about finances and not innovation work, I find author Nassim Taleb's barbell strategy helpful. He suggested that sensible risk-taking is one where, should the worst happen, the business will be able to cope with it, but the potential upside is extraordinary or uncapped. Let us translate this to innovation. Capping the downside means that you should not invest too much work into a direction that has not proven its utility yet, and strive to have feedback cycles that are as short as possible. Otherwise, you might realize that you spent hundreds of thousands of dollars and have nothing to show for it.

The other part is about picking bets that can genuinely make a dent in your business. For many tech teams, this part is harder to assess. I have seen many cases where teams thought a creative solution they had for simplifying a particular process was great, only for the executive team to shrug their shoulders and say it was not painful enough. The problem is that this shrugging usually occurs *after* the team has implemented the change. Placing the right sort of barbell bets requires the team to articulate what benefits their ideas might bring and talk about them in business terms with the related stakeholders. Only thus can they ensure that they are not heading in a direction no one cares about.

A great example would be PayPal's innovation program.[2] It is about making employees wager about which innovation directions they think are most likely to succeed while focusing on business needs. The first iteration of their program already yielded significant improvements in average customer-handling times and loads.

The wanted result is an organization where engineers do not spend disproportionate amounts of time on a direction with little value or risk a different part of the roadmap that is critical. Nevertheless, bets are bets, and even the best teams should fail sometimes. Those cases have to be handled properly as well.

Embracing Failures

One final part of cultivating an innovative hothouse is accepting the nature of genuine innovation, which is its uncertainty. The worst thing about kicking off initiatives for creativity is for the executive team to get angry and disappointed when some ideas inevitably hit a dead end. When this happens, your team is not likely to confront you. Instead, they will simply learn that to cover their bases, they mustn't attempt anything short of a sure win. Your following intermissions would bring diminishing value as teams will merely go through the motions of creativity.

Most anything that is genuinely innovative and novel is not guaranteed to work. Accept that this is the case and set your expectations accordingly. You should feel fine about inevitable misses as long as you see a regular stream of tangible results with the business focus already covered. I would go even further and say that one would do well to give a pat on the back to those who came up with a good idea that did not work out.

It is worth noting that not all failures are final. While some of the experiments might end up with a final verdict that the idea is futile, some can continue to evolve. By riffing on an idea that did not quite work out, the team might find another path to success or repurpose some tool to achieve a different result. Thus, even the failures are valuable as the team learns from them and leverages the accumulated knowledge to improve future iterations.

ACTION ITEMS

There is not a company that cannot benefit from more innovation. To make innovation habitual in your organization, start with these steps:

- Assess your current innovation and measure it.
- Determine which parts of the R&D group are the best for starting with intermissions.
- Schedule your first intermissions.
- Evaluate whether a dedicated research team or task force is called for.

NOTES

1. For more resources about intermissions, you can direct your tech team to: https://techexecutiveoperatingsystem.com/.
2. See how PayPal gets employees invested in innovation, *Harvard Business Review.* https://hbr.org/2022/07/how-paypal-gets-employees-invested-in-innovation.

7

Making R&D Transparent and Predictable: Handling the Soft Parts of Software

Anyone that has ever worked with tech teams has experienced at least once the dreaded infinite project. Those projects act like Zeno's paradoxes: whenever you try to figure out the project's status, it seems to be in the last 20% of the work declared in the previous status check, as Figure 7.1 illustrates. Deadlines keep getting postponed and delayed, sometimes even *after* they have passed. You find out that even more people are needed to achieve something simpler than what the team initially agreed to.

This pattern of death march projects is very common—*too common*—and happens even at organizations with talented and experienced teams that previously operated well. Changes in company culture, communication overhead, and lack of connection to the product can result in projects that feel like wandering through the desert for 40 years. Unsurprisingly, the executive team rarely puts up with such behavior for long. After this has taken place once or twice, they pull their sleeves up.

When burned, most leaders then move to higher engagement and closer inspection. They ask for more details. They poke around and question decisions and reports. They might get involved in operational decisions. In short, they start micromanaging. Micromanagement is something that most experienced managers are aware of and hate doing. However, most of us hate missing deadlines and failing to hit our objectives even more. Therefore, when the trust in the team has been damaged, leadership turns to keep them on a tighter leash.

There is bad news and good news. The bad news is that even with micromanagement, things rarely improve sufficiently and require too

DOI: 10.4324/9781003358473-7

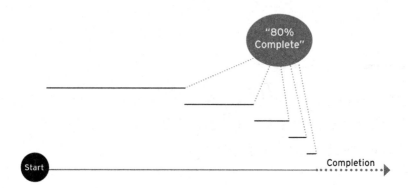

FIGURE 7.1
Zeno's paradox of the never-ending project.

much attention from the management and senior staff that other areas suffer. The good news is that there are better ways to solve this.

SOFTWARE DEVELOPMENT MANAGEMENT

Tons of books, certifications, and conference talks have been created around the different approaches to managing software delivery. One can hardly get within ten feet of a software engineer without hearing about Scrum, agile, or sprints. Before getting down in the weeds with the meaning of these different buzzwords and how they affect you, let us start by ensuring that you view things correctly.

Delivery Cycles Affect the Entire Company

While many tech teams believe their delivery processes are mostly an internal matter, that couldn't be farther from the truth. I have seen companies where the software organization was attempting to push new versions out rapidly, which was harmful to the business. I have also witnessed the opposite, where tech teams were operating in a way that was too slow for the business's needs. If you are afraid that asking to talk about the software delivery cadence is micromanagement, don't be.

In fact, most agile methodologies claim that "real agile" requires the involvement of the entire company. Many teams would only be so lucky to have their executive team care about such matters. The cadence has to match your industry, your clients' needs, and the company's objectives. For example, when working on a direction that has yet to be validated, the teams shouldn't go off to work on something and resurface only six months later. That precious time could have been used to gather feedback and ensure the project was headed in the right direction.

CASE STUDY: THE HANDCUFFED CEO

The CEO of a nontraditional startup was unhappy with the way software development was progressing. The tech managers were dogmatic and shut down any attempt to change the cadence or have higher visibility and flexibility so the executive team could focus on getting its first paying clients. The CEO told me, "I felt helpless. The team made me think that any request I made immediately meant we were operating in Waterfall[1] mode like it's the 70s and that all our senior engineers would leave." Like two people with unsynchronized watches, the business, and the tech team kept missing the other. The business people required transparency and certain features for proofs of concept. The tech team expected certain decisions to be made at times that didn't match the sales process.

When I started advising their executive team, one of the first things we tackled was the software cadence. We helped everyone in the company understand that this was the company's heartbeat and had to match everyone's needs. We stopped using buzzwords to describe the process. Instead, we defined goals and intentions and built a bespoke process based on agreed-upon principles so that every ritual and meeting had clear reasoning behind it. No one was cargo-culting what they saw in blog posts.

Cut to today, and things are much better. Even though the organization has grown tenfold since we implemented these measures, the company never slowed down. It is now a successful unicorn that delivers smoothly both regular software updates and innovative research-driven novelties. The CEO said, "I needed you to give me permission to get involved and demand what makes sense for us. Once I felt it was okay, we could keep adjusting the process as we grew and our needs changed."

No One-Size-Fits-All Process

There are two crucial and slightly contrasting aspects when deciding how to structure the team's processes. First, do not attempt to invent everything from scratch. It makes a lot of sense to see what common patterns there are and what others have tried and learn from collective experience. This is where you can easily stand on the shoulders of giants and save your company from reinventing the wheel.

The second aspect is to never dogmatically copy another company's scheme. Starting from a certain template is logical, but expect to change it regularly and almost immediately. The tension between the two is when teams allow themselves to disregard common wisdom too easily by giving some hand-waving explanation that they are different or when they stick to a specific "rule" even when it clearly makes no sense to them.

Thus, you would do well to rely on the experience of senior staff and even consult external experts. Do so while ensuring that no party treats its favorable methodology as the one true way—sacrosanct for any change to be considered. Personally, I recommend my clients avoid bringing in anyone with a certification in any specific methodology unless they have vetted them for being open-minded. Zealots rarely have great results.

Common Approaches and Their Strengths/Weaknesses

Given that most companies tend to start with one of the more common methodologies as a basis and start tailoring and adjusting from that, one would do well to understand the differences and intentions of the most popular methodologies. This is intended more as a glossary to help you realize where intervention might be necessary and why certain "rules" seem to apply.

Agile: The grandparent methodology. After the waterfall model was debunked in the late 1990s, a group of software enthusiasts met and created the Agile Manifesto. It kicked off a whole new generation of better, faster software delivery. Agile is not a single methodology but a set of principles and mindsets from which many other methodologies have emerged. Thus, two companies can be agile and yet operate differently.

When I described above that companies would do well to decide on principles and have their processes flow from them, I had something like the agile manifesto in mind. It has statements like "we value individuals and interactions over processes and tools" or "responding to change over following a plan." Most companies would do well to mold an agile-inspired process to fit their needs.

Do note that there is a profusion of certifications and training courses for "Agile" frameworks. While getting trained is not a bad thing, many have grown weary of these so-called "capital-A Agile" methodologies. Again, avoid zealots and go for something that accepts customization.

Scrum: By far the most common agile approach in startups. When a team uses Scrum, it usually has a few characteristic rituals. Work is performed in iterations or sprints that often take 2–3 weeks. Every sprint is planned, so the team has a tangible deliverable to show by the end. Sprints start with a sprint planning or kickoff session. They end with demos and a retrospective where the team debriefs and attempts to learn from how things went. Usually, every day the teams meet for a few minutes to stay in sync. This is called the "daily Scrum" or the "daily standup" (often abbreviated as "daily" or "standup"). The dailies are the heartbeat of the engineering team, while the iterations form the heartbeat of product releases.

Some larger organizations might have "Scrum masters," who are often individual contributors who take on extra responsibilities as part of the sprint to ensure that everything is running smoothly. These are essentially process champions that help guide the team and track how well the methodology is being executed. There are troves of certifications and training programs for these "certified Scrum masters." Unless the team already has someone with the experience, do not fret about it. It is perfectly fine (sometimes even better) to start with your engineering managers taking this responsibility as part of their roles.

Kanban: Similar to Scrum, yet different. Kanban is adapted from a Japanese manufacturing process that focuses on lowering bottlenecks and actively monitoring the entire flow of software engineering to ensure that the most important and valuable task is being performed at any given point. Kanban often operates without set iterations or sprints. Work is constantly released and whatever is ready is "pushed to production." This is a double-edged sword: there is less planning overhead, and the team can more nimbly move to whatever is the most pressing need. It is also harder to ensure that a strategic direction is followed, and software releases can seem more random.

In my experience, Kanban works better for smaller, research-driven teams. These are teams where a longer-term roadmap might not be relevant, and customer needs are still being uncovered. Similarly, it lends itself more to B2C products or B2B SaaS companies, where updates are often done without much large fanfare or hassle for customers to update. While releasing software continuously can happen in other methodologies as well, for Kanban, it is par for the course.

A word of warning: Kanban is often harder for inexperienced teams to manage effectively due to its flexibility. I would say that only about 20% of the groups I have seen using it stuck with it for over a year. The lack of clear deadlines in the form of sprints can harm the team's cadence. We will cover that later.

Measuring Agility

There are a few terms often used in agile to describe how effective the team is and spot issues early on. While teams do not necessarily track all of them, keeping at least one in mind is a good way to ensure that productivity problems do not go unnoticed for too long.

Velocity: A measure of how fast the team delivers new work. It is often measured as the number of features/tasks/user stories released per given time period. Sometimes measured in "story points" (e.g., a minor feature is a single point while a more complicated one could be a five or a seven).

Cycle time: The time it takes since work on an item starts until it is completed. Since cycle time tracks the wall-clock time since work has begun, it can help shine a light on cases where there is too much work in progress, and thus, things get stuck and delayed for too long. Think of cycle time as tracking how long since you asked for a particular dish in a restaurant until you got it. If it takes too long because the kitchen is swamped, you might no longer be hungry by the time you get it.

Burn-down: Less common nowadays, burn-down charts track the team's progress toward a particular milestone. For example, a sprint starts with 30 features and tasks and has 10 workdays. Thus, the team would ideally close three items daily to stay on track. A burn-down chart helps spot when the team is starting to lag behind.

Figure 7.2 shows how these different charts often look.

Choosing Your Agile Principles

A healthy discussion with your tech leadership about the software delivery process should revolve around the most important principles for the

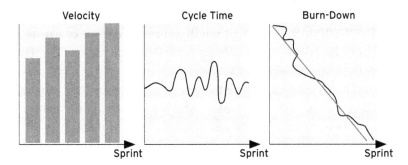

FIGURE 7.2
Different sprint progress charts.

company. Define your needs and ideal culture in terms that will provide guidance to tailor the proper methodology. Here are some common suggestions for healthy agile principles.

Incremental iterations: One of the most impactful concepts of agile development is that we let go of the hope of ever conjuring a "perfect" solution, especially in one "go." One of the critical fallacies of the waterfall model was that teams would attempt to design a solution that is just right, driven by the belief that if one spends enough time in the planning phases of the project, the rest of the work will flow smoothly. However, that tends to be a waste of effort.

Past a certain level of planning and research, the marginal benefit of every extra day spent contemplating the ideal solution goes down rapidly. The complexity of modern systems, coupled with the rapid changes in the market and unknown variables that can only be revealed by getting a product out in people's hands, means that attempting to conjure a flawless plan is futile. Therefore, you are far better off agreeing to work in short cycles and adjusting course as you go along.

Do note that while iterations make it harder to get the team to commit to a hard deadline a few months into the future, doing so with rigid planning is even more likely to fail. Iterations mean that at least there is a regular cadence for checking the team's progress toward the goal. Otherwise, many teams realize they are not going to make it only in the final stretch. Iterations make the team live with Parkinson's law[2] every couple of weeks but on a smaller scale than bundling it all up to the end of a three-month project.

Incorporate feedback diligently: Let us refer back to the house construction example from the first chapter. When we left the construction crew on its own for several months, they inevitably started drifting from our vision. Such drifts and small misalignments are a law of nature and will occur in every scenario involving more than one person. The trick is to put tight feedback loops in place.

Feedback loops are cycles where those producing display their progress to stakeholders and customers and assess whether they are on the right track. Coupling this with iterations creates a straightforward point to inject this feedback. Once one iteration is completed and before the team dives into the next, demos for key personnel and users can provide precious insights. The proper mechanism for gathering this feedback changes between teams, but without it, your R&D group is guaranteed to get lost eventually. Would you rather find out a week after it happened or at the end of the quarter?

Speak value: At every turn, the discussion should revolve around the results you want to achieve and the benefit to customers. We tend to focus on the bits and the bytes of tasks once we start working on them. Thus we quickly lose sight of what we wanted to achieve. Frequently, this disconnect is how teams end up creating solutions that might be technical marvels yet disconnected from the clients' needs.

The exact value of every feature—the reason this endeavor is worth it for the business—should be discussed from the kickoff. Ideally, the team should be given an objective to achieve, not a prescriptive set of tasks, and the autonomy to decide on the best path to reach that goal. When privy to the value chain, they are more likely to focus their creativity on that. Geeks are bound to have hair-splitting discussions about minutiae. We might as well have these benefit the users as opposed to coming up with technical solutions that are too complex.

Default to sooner: As the team progresses in its works and more iterations unfold toward a goal, changes will creep up. Perhaps you will learn that a problem is more complicated than you initially assumed and will require more effort to solve. A beta client may suggest an improvement to an existing feature to make it even more valuable to them. Whatever the case is, avoid increasing the scope of the work prematurely. This is known as *scope creep*, which is why many deadlines worldwide get thrown to the sidelines every week.

There are good ideas everywhere, but turning your development process into a high-tech version of the never-ending story is not a good idea. Instead, the team should default to sitting on its hands a bit before committing to any additional work. Unless there is a very clear reason why a suggestion merits changing the plan, it should be added to the *backlog* and reviewed at a later point. This way, the team can deliver something and get feedback on it instead of having to push back the demo or release every time because there is "just one more thing" to do.

I once saw a startup that had a promising direction create its first version of its product with some beta clients already signed up and waiting to get the first version in their hands. Somehow along the way, the entire team seemed to have lost sight of the value they were looking to create, as well as allowing themselves repeatedly to go into do-overs and make minor tweaks to what they were working on. They spent over a year in this limbo without fully realizing that they were preventing themselves from getting to the market and getting access to the detailed feedback they needed to escape this trap. Only with a kick in the rear in the form of an ever-smaller balance in the bank did they wake up and put a stop to the incessant scope creep.

USING DEADLINES CORRECTLY

Many executives and startup founders that want to pose deadlines on product engineering goals might be surprised at the pushback they receive. Many tech leaders vehemently reject the concept of using "arbitrary deadlines" in order to stress the team into work. Even your technical cofounders might be opposed to it. What is that all about?

We are the sum of our experiences, and many senior techies have had a whole bunch of negative experiences with stress-inducing bosses in the past. After having to burn the midnight oil too often for no real reason, they might have promised themselves that they would never be like that as managers. Especially for those logically inclined, the idea of rushing to get something done by a date merely because "someone said so" can feel idiotic. Nevertheless, as part of our effort to make R&D predictable and to have it work with the rest of the company, we need to learn how to put them into use.

Bad Deadlines

I don't know you, dear reader, and therefore cannot tell whether you are the type of person that might be more prone to abuse deadlines. Thus, I have the duty of ensuring you can tell which management practices might be common yet tend to achieve the opposite of a healthy and productive team. While we will soon cover how deadlines can be used to the team's benefit, we have to talk about how deadlines get their bad rap.

Arbitrary deadlines are those where the team commits to finishing some grand project by a specific date merely because the executive team decided that this date is when things should be done. What if I told you that you must finish a marathon in one hour tomorrow? No matter how committed you were to the "cause" and tried your best to put in some training and stretching before it starts, you are bound to fail. As ridiculous as that sounds, that is how many companies operate. The management team comes up with an initiative, decides when it would be "nice" to have it ready, and then shoves those deadlines down people's throats until people have agreed to do it on the surface.

What actually takes place is that everyone believes that the goal is unreal yet starts working toward it. They might work extra because they care and would like to minimize how late the work ends up being. Nevertheless, they would not be surprised when two weeks before the end date, everything is still far from being ready. Only the executive team is genuinely surprised— they thought everyone was committed to that deadline.

Even worse, sometimes the teams actually do make those deadlines work. They work extra hard. They cut corners and amass genuine tech debt. Sometimes when they succeed, it doesn't even matter. Since the deadline was arbitrary, the business might require several more weeks to actually start using the new product. No matter when it is used, another feedback cycle is at play here. The executive team just learned that it is possible to crunch the team into blitz mode and get what they wanted.

The company's leadership is oblivious to the cost: the sleepless nights, the bad quality work that the team had to push out and are not proud of, and the weeks of mounting pressure and stress. Not seeing all this, they repeat the process. Eventually, something breaks—the people or the product being built ever more flimsily. This is precisely what your team is afraid of happening. Do not be this manager.

The Benefits of Deadlines

The first part of making the team open to more rigid deadlines is to help them see the value in using them. Making your case is critical. Here are the common arguments I use to help teams.

Predictability is necessary: Even if the deadlines themselves are arbitrary—meaning they are self-imposed—having confidence in them is highly valuable. Every company needs to be able to orchestrate more significant projects across the entire organization. For example, if the team does not commit to when a particular capability will be ready, how can the marketing and growth teams prepare their campaigns to waste minimal time? Without knowing when a change is likely to be done, the salespeople cannot promise it to prospects, and customer success would not be able to give clients affected by bugs estimates of resolution.

Manage appetites: We will touch on this in more depth later in this chapter, but the concept is that you want to control the work investment and cap it to how important something is. Merely telling the team that you want X done and asking for their estimate often results in superfluous solutions. When you start by stating your "appetite" for a certain need, e.g., by saying you are willing to have the team invest about two weeks in it, you put in place a constraint that helps shape the chosen solution.[3]

This is not about arbitrarily telling the team to do something by an impossible deadline but about providing business value as guidance. They can and should speak up if they believe that time is not enough to implement a solution that will achieve the company's goals. But just as your overall budget guides which house you will purchase and what type of car you will be in the market for, your appetite will help you find the best solution.

Overcoming Parkinson's law: Lastly, there is nothing wrong with being honest. It is human nature to have tasks take longer than needed. Having a due date helps focus efforts and coordinate cross-team collaboration. Telling the team that at least part of the benefit of deadlines is that they help them get things done is perfectly fine.

Leveraging Deadlines

We have seen that deadlines can result in burnout and low quality. To avoid that, their introduction into your company's processes has to address these pitfalls. The first part is to understand the triangle of software delivery. See Figure 7.3.

The old adage says that one must choose solely two aspects from the triangle. For example, you can have a fast and complete solution but at low quality or a comprehensive and high-quality solution that takes time.

FIGURE 7.3
The triangle of software delivery.

When putting deadlines in place, management cannot fix all three aspects of the triangle. In fact, deciding which single aspect is most important is often better to help direct the team's approach.

Therefore, if you have a critical deadline with external obligations to reach, you treat that as a constant, and the team adjusts the scope and quality of the solution to reach that time-based deadline. In other cases, the work might have demanding regulatory standards meaning that the scope and quality are rigid. In those scenarios, you can only reach genuine buy-in from the time by letting them determine the time required to implement such a solution.

Also, keep in mind that any organization has hierarchies of deadlines. The biggest one is the roadmap-based deadline, such as a commitment to deliver a big product by the end of the quarter. It comprises many smaller deadlines, such as commitments to have specific work finished by each sprint in the quarter. Those sprints might have smaller deadlines, as some teams hold the R&D engineers accountable for their effort estimates to some degree. Some teams do great at one level but worse at others. If you spot such an issue, it often indicates that the triangle is not considered at that resolution.

Addressing the Language Barrier

One last typical pitfall when using deadlines is how a deadline might mean one thing to you and a different one entirely to those working on the task. Consider a scenario where you ask that a certain change be done by a specific date. While you might have meant that as general guidance, the team interpreted it as a hard date that cannot be missed. That brought them to work into the night and cut corners during the last week. When you find out (if at all), you might say that had they told you, you could have explained that a couple extra days wouldn't be problematic. However, that is already too late, and the damage is done. The team has worked hard, but the quality delivered is lower than expected, and you will have to spend extra time fixing that.

Other teams have it the other way around. Years of seeing how deadlines meant nothing because after they were done, the company still required weeks to go to clients have taught them to treat deadlines as a general guideline. Whenever you assign a due date, the team has to know how *rigid* that date is. That way, the team can tailor a solution correctly and avoid surprises.

DEFINE APPETITES

An interesting approach to prioritizing product development is to flip the time estimates on their head. Many default to listing features and letting the engineers dictate how long it will take to implement them. The appetite concept is about stakeholders saying how much they would like to invest in these features. Whereas many create deadlines by asking the team for an estimate and then holding it accountable to it, appetites state the time frame and goal and ask the group what can be achieved during that time.

The difference might seem semantic, but it can direct the whole organization on a healthier path. When stakeholders ask for things to be done, their "currency" internally is how much they are willing to invest in the solution, most significantly in the form of team time. When a change is only deemed worth a couple of days, everyone can easily infer that it is not a strategic direction, but more of a housekeeping need. On the other hand, an initiative that is assigned to a team for an entire quarter is much more important. Stating your appetite makes you put your money where your mouth is.

It is a more advanced approach, requiring tighter cooperation and a better understanding of the work needed. After all, if your appetites are always comically optimistic, they are not helpful to the discussion. Nevertheless, it should be considered as it tends to form better relationships across the company and increase transparency.

NO RADIO SILENCE

It is funny how much human beings seem to like tracking numbers. As much as ordering things online is fun, it is sometimes even more satisfying to keep track of items as they work their way to us. We regularly pay more for shipping with a tracking number, even if it doesn't affect the delivery date. That is because we simply *want to know* what is going on. This transparency has a lot of value. It makes us more relaxed because we can tell that progress is being made steadily and that things are still on track.

Making an R&D organization predictable has a similar requirement. When teams go into "radio silence" and don't keep others apprised of progress, doubt grows. The longer the silence period, the worse the anxiety seems to be. Those doing the work frequently do not realize this. From their point of view, they can see the work made and the daily progress. They fail to grasp how communicating it is needed to make other parties relaxed as well.

Set Up Regular "Resurfacing" Points

There is no doubt that there is a lot of value in increased transparency, even if it does not result in any changes to the actual work. By setting the others in the company at ease, R&D slowly accumulates more trust. That trust will later be translated into freedom to invest in initiatives, change directions, or even simply to loop engineers in more often.

Further, the act of communicating the current state and progress to nontechnical counterparts also tends to save the tech team precious time. Instead of operating in silence and getting capricious requests for status reports from all directions at seemingly random times, your tech leadership can take hold of these status meetings. Thus, they can have a single status meeting instead of having dozens of smaller ones. The content of those also tends to be better articulated as there is an opportunity to prepare for a pre-scheduled meeting. That is not the same when one of the engineers is tackled in the hall, unaware by some senior manager that asks for an update. I cannot count how many times I saw companies' alarm bells go off because an engineer answered a question at the water cooler with an answer that worried everyone but was merely misunderstood (or incorrect).

Solve this by ensuring that the team's process loops in all relevant stakeholders at intervals that make sense. It might be a monthly high-level overview of the entire R&D group's progress, and you might set up a specific update for a high-risk project that takes place twice a week. If you feel anxious, don't be afraid to ask for more updates.

Inject Feedback and Prevent Drift

Similarly, these communication touch points can even be more helpful by involving deliberate feedback. You do not want to see a situation where these statuses become entirely unidirectional: R&D throws up a bunch of data, and everyone else sits and nods until the clock shows they're free to go to their next meeting. Whenever a tech team begins a new effort, it regularly drifts apart from the stakeholders and customers as time passes. Ideally, at the moment of initiation, they were in sync, but it is possible that things were misunderstood already at that stage.

As work progresses, the engineers' vision of business needs and customers gets cloudy. What they heard in the initial discussions slowly fades. That is because they are focusing on hundreds of technical decisions, and each changes that vision, even if slightly. The longer the team is allowed to remain in radio silence, the more it will diverge. Figure 7.4 illustrates the difference in drift with and without feedback. If the team has months between getting feedback, course correction at that point will be an expensive and time-consuming effort. Instead, inject stakeholder feedback in an ongoing manner. Corrections are a lot easier to make if they are noticed early on.

Status meetings and update emails that go smoothly, without any questions or even merely reinforcements, guarantee that sooner or later, a major issue will be revealed where all sides pass the blame to the others. After all, they "told you!" When I see a CEO sitting in one of these monthly updates and constantly checking email and not taking part in the meeting, I usually suggest canceling the meeting altogether. The CEO is always incredulous—but I point out how the meeting is certainly not worth their attention and feedback. I've yet to see a client not promise to change their

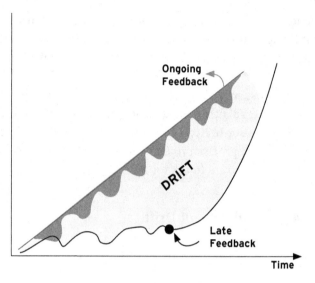

FIGURE 7.4
Feedback drift.

ways, but some never really do. Put your attention where your mouth is. If needed, make the meetings shorter or ask that they are communicated in a less technical and dry manner. Whatever it takes, meetings need to include lively discussion to maximize all of their potential gains.

ACTION ITEMS

Creating transparency and predictability is a long-term effort that often has to be intensified as the team evolves and becomes more complex. No matter what stage you are at, consider doing the following:

- Review your existing processes based on the guidelines listed and your business needs.
- Have an open discussion with your tech leaders about how deadlines are used in the company and whether a change in approach is needed.
- Establish regular status touch points with affected parties to increase communication and reduce anxiety.
- Consider whether your current status meetings prevent drift and inject enough feedback or should something be changed.

NOTES

1. Waterfall model is the name of a process where each step of software development is very rigorous and has to be completed before moving to the next in serial progression. It is very different from the incremental nature of modern software delivery and is frowned upon. See https://en.wikipedia.org/wiki/Waterfall_model.
2. "Work expands so as to fill the time available for its completion." See https://en.wikipedia.org/wiki/Parkinson's_law.
3. Calling these constraints "appetites" is based on the Shape Up approach; see https://basecamp.com/shapeup.

8

Injecting Chutzpah: Culture Lessons from the World's Unicorn Capital

By this point, you might have spotted a repeating motive: I assume that given enough product knowledge, your tech team will speak up. They will let you know of possible problems and their innovative ideas, all culminating in a nexus of creativity and productivity. I do not intend to paint a picture that it is as easy as that. There is an essential cultural ingredient that we often lack: *chutzpah*.

When I first started working with companies outside of Israel, I had a hard time realizing this. While everywhere I worked previously had this ability innately, that was not the case in many other organizations. Like fish always noticing the water last, it took me time to realize that what I had taken for granted is not always straightforward for others. Chutzpah is often cited as one of the reasons for Israel's tech success. You can transplant chutzpah into your organization with some cultural cultivation.

WHAT DOES IT EVEN MEAN?

Before you get all stressed about having to learn to pronounce this weird word correctly, let us define what we are talking about. Here is my definition of chutzpah in a business context:

CHUTZPAH /ˈxʊtspə/ NOUN:

The quality of grit and audacity to speak one's mind and be candid regardless of rank, politics, and emotions.

DOI: 10.4324/9781003358473-8

Consider the fable *The Emperor's New Clothes*. There, only the innocent and somewhat tactless child could speak up and say that the emperor is not wearing anything. Many modern organizations, big and small, seem to be stuck in the same situation. Unfortunately, most do not employ kids and therefore have no one to break the spell.

Think back to one of your recent company all-hands. Did they include questions that genuinely poked at the company's current direction or how it measured its progress? What was the last time someone pointed out that your competitors were doing something much better? We talked about the problems of teams going into order-taking mode. The opposite is a team that works hard to wrap its head around the goals before moving forward. To grok things, chutzpah is often necessary.

Those with enough chutzpah have the grit to persevere, question assumptions, and suggest different viewpoints. They do not stop after the first time that their questions were answered glibly.

Not Insubordination

Funny enough, while *chutzpah* as a Yiddishism has come to mean that positive audacity, here in Israel, it is used differently. In everyday Hebrew, chutzpah is the equivalent of rudeness or insolence. And indeed, there is a fine line between the two definitions. It is not hard to imagine how someone might overdo their chutzpah practice to a point where it is disadvantageous.

For example, I am sure you have met that cynical engineer that seems to automatically shoot down all ideas and deflate any new initiative. Or those that lack the ability to "disagree and commit"—they will keep raising objections at every single step along the way. Such behavior, even when well intended, ends up making things almost unbearable. One would have to be a saint to manage such an employee and never lose one's temper.

When we talk about cultivating chutzpah, we aim for the sweet spot. Fortunately for us, it is quite a substantial target. Many teams are so lacking anyone willing to speak up that they should be afraid of overshooting all the way to people being cheeky without anyone noticing it. Funny enough, I have frequently seen teams that had no one with healthy audacity and a handful of senior engineers that serve as embitterment ambassadors. Making others speak up actually tends to reduce this bitter cynicism.

The Benefits

Have you ever seen a team fail to do something only to realize later that the engineers knew the direction was wrong but kept silent? The dreaded "you never asked me" makes an appearance, and everyone has a postmortem full of face-palming. *Not fun.*

Sometimes after companies publicly acknowledge that a specific strategy was unsuccessful, journalists surface many stories of those on the inside that knew all along. They often recount how they felt no one "higher up" was connected to the team and their fears. That is precisely the type of scenario *chutzpah* should help you evade. It means that people will speak up more freely and not let you go in the wrong direction merely out of some weird sense of obedience, fear of being frank, or "respect" for authority.

When enough safety is created to encourage open discourse, you get even more benefits aside from the actual problems you avoid. First, the team members are keeping fewer things to themselves. The ability to vent regularly releases pressure and makes everyone less "explosive." Arguments do not go nuclear as often, and you get fewer people who leave the company without any warning.

If you've ever had to go through a social event where you felt as if you had to put on a display and be overly politically correct, you know what a relief it was to finally go home afterward. We do not want employees to feel like that. If one is too busy putting on a facade, too much of the brain's creativity and cognitive ability are lost to it.

Another benefit is how much stress this open culture removes from decision-makers. When no one speaks up, many decisions are made in a void, without a good debate to help ensure everything is considered. This lack of feedback is the cause of decision-waffling in many organizations. Leaders keep waiting for some extra input that never arrives. In *chutzpah*-forward organizations, though, this is not the issue. Putting bruised egos aside, immediate and clear feedback facilitates more rapid decisions. You can point in a direction to charge and know that if there is a pitfall ahead or a better path, someone will let you know.

A UNIT OF RADICAL CHUTZPAH

Many attribute the high ratio of unicorns per capita in Israel to our army's tech units and the experience many get there every year. If that is the case, then indeed, the Israeli tendency to disregard authority plays a role in it. Right from my first months as a programmer, I witnessed how even the newest recruits were being heard. Ideas and suggestions were rarely dismissed immediately.

I cannot count how many times incredible feats were accomplished merely because someone was not afraid to speak up about a crazy idea half-jokingly and see it considered. While I cannot share classified details, I think the circumstances can help visualize what such an organization feels like quotidianly.

First, many times creativity was maximized when all of the brilliant people in the room were able to participate in brainstorming fully. When no one is too shy to suggest an idea, you eventually get some mind-boggling out-of-the-box ideas. I have since likened it to watching a professional improv session where each person continues from where the previous one left off, picking up more and more steam.

Second, we saved gobs of time going in the wrong directions because no one silently nodded and moved along. We poked and prodded until we felt the plan made sense to us. One example that comes to mind is how, as a corporal, I told a lieutenant general his idea was nonsensical, and he simply listened and accepted it. Another time, we were integrating with a different unit, and the programmer I worked with, which I barely knew, was having trouble solving things on his end. With a bit of nerve, I asked to come to his office and look at the code together, even though it was in a programming language I didn't know. I quickly ended up taking control of the keyboard and solving the issue (after that, my teammates said I was the best person at integrating with myself).

I have since learned that a potent inhibitor of creativity is the *common sense filter* that many of us apply to our thinking silently. We assume that most ideas we have are trivial, and therefore were they worth mentioning, someone else would have done so already. The ability to ask another person a question that might seem trivial can spare a lot of time. In the examples above, I could have just shrugged and presumed that the other party had considered everything I had, but I didn't. That bit of *chutzpah* saves a lot of time in aggregate. Stop filtering common sense.

UNDERSTANDING SCARCITY

If these examples of positive audacity have triggered your thinking to spot cases where the exact opposite has happened in your company, know that you are not alone. Many organizations suffer from a chutzpah deficiency. It is not limited to tech teams, though the tech-business language barrier tends to make it more commonplace. Every team is different and might have diverse factors inhibiting how outspoken and open the communication is. In fact, it varies individually. Understanding the common causes for the scarcity of chutzpah and how to spot them can aid your management team in cultivating it.

Cultural Misconceptions

One type of chutzpah blocker is all about the different cultural viewpoints in the company. Some might be unique to your company, and others are more prevalent. For example, some companies seem to prioritize authority and hierarchy over collaboration and candor. If you have a culture of secrecy or of holding a grudge whenever someone questions a decision from "higher up," you cannot be surprised when no one speaks up.

On the other end of the spectrum are misconceptions not caused by your company but by the environments and backgrounds of your employees. When I spoke about chutzpah in conferences and interviews worldwide, I often got skeptical questions from those concerned about political correctness in the United States or about conforming to hierarchy in Asia. There are countless stories of managers who first worked with employees or contractors from other cultures and realized too late that their requests were immediately accepted, even when the team knew they made no sense. Spotting that this is an issue within your company is critical to be able to address it.

Lack of Agency

It can sometimes seem utterly irrational to bystanders when people follow nonsensical orders, even when their instincts are all telling them something is wrong. You might have seen those documentaries about aviation accidents that portray how the younger, less experienced copilot knew something was awry but did not speak up before it was too late. We do not even have to go to extremes. Not a week goes by without a CEO telling me how they would *love* to see their people, often senior executives included, come to them less asking for guidance and instead taking the initiative. "I don't want to tell my staff what to do; I want them to come up to me with ideas" is something I hear regularly.

This sort of silence can often be traced back to issues of agency or psychological safety. Before covering the latter, you should know how to spot agency problems. When people do not speak up because they do not have enough autonomy, they usually have a core belief that it is not their role to do so. This is not related to fear but some genuine feeling that there is a "box" that they are in and that speaking up is not within the confines of their job description. Often, those self-erected boundaries have no real connection to the real world and are adhered to much to the chagrin of their managers.

This is where the "you didn't ask" reply comes from: they honestly thought their opinion was irrelevant. Sometimes this happens due to the company's culture, but on many occasions, I've seen this be entirely about how some people view the world by default. It is not uncommon to see startup teams where part of the team assumes agency and autonomy while other team members do not.

CASE STUDY: REJECTING "STARTUP" CULTURE

Going back more than a decade, I was the first employee in a new startup. We were a handful of very young software engineers, and for most of us, this was our first startup, including the CTO. For the first two months, we did what we saw on TV: we worked extremely hard. We were regularly in the office for about 12 hours, day in and day out. It was exhausting for everyone. In hindsight, I think we were sucked into some herd mentality, where each felt that this was simply the way things were.

After two months of this, one night, as I was driving home, I fell asleep at the wheel for a split second. Fortunately, nothing happened, but I knew things had to change. The next day, I came in and said I cannot work that way anymore and will scale down to "normal" hours or leave. No one batted an eye. A week or two later, the rest of the team was putting in the same hours as I was.

The team did not become less productive. It got faster. When you are not stuck in your seat for hours on end, you value your time more. You might as well finish things faster so you can go home earlier. Contrast that with knowing you will be there until 9 p.m. no matter what—there is no rush. Why did none of us speak up? We had a lot of agency when it came to the product itself and the technology, but we assumed the work atmosphere was just how startups operated. It took a life-risking drive home to help me fix things.

No Psychological Safety

The other common trait that is required for effective chutzpah is psychological safety. A Google research team famously surveyed their most effective groups in search of the critical ingredients of top teams and ranked psychological safety as the most crucial factor.[1] Psychological safety means that one feels that the team is a safe space where there is no danger of making foolish comments, speaking up, and making mistakes in general.

In teams where no one feels there is room for any mistakes, people tend to put their heads down and merely *execute.* Just as we saw how accepting failures is required for innovation, it is essential to create a safe environment for people to speak their minds. Leaders that have a tendency to "shoot the messenger" or belittle anyone that makes a lousy suggestion push all psychological safety out of the room and risk forming legions of yes-people who never question anything (at least not out loud).

CULTIVATING CHUTZPAH

By this point, we have covered the importance of chutzpah in high-performing teams and its common inhibitors. The question is, which steps should you take as a senior executive to enable such a culture within your R&D team (and throughout the company, really)? I am happy to say you do not have to limit yourself to hiring Israelis or opening offices in Tel Aviv (though if you do, let's grab coffee). There are a few simple tactics that I have seen managers successfully apply to increase how candid their teams are.

Give Permission

The first step, as straightforward as it might seem, is to regularly give people permission to speak up, question the current thinking, and suggest different directions. Merely stating this as part of your company values and plastering it on the wall is not enough. It is something that should be part of your regular meeting practices.

For example, it is practically ubiquitous as executives to claim you are always open to feedback and have an "open door policy." The problem with these doors is that they seem to be seldom walked through. The friction for speaking up, especially for the first time, is too high for many. Therefore, executives have to work harder to make this happen in general, and specifically with newer employees. Especially when in touch with individual contributors, proactively tease out feedback and ask for their opinion. Consider these phrases that give specific permission and encourage speaking up:

- "… and that is our current plan for this quarter. Now, tell me, what here surprises you?"
- "Please question what we just presented. Just because we showed it on slides does not make it gospel, and we would rather spot our mistakes sooner than later."
- "So it seems like everyone that participated so far agrees with our direction. If someone thinks differently, I'd love to hear different takes."
- "Any questions about this update? Letting me know what you think is not merely encouraged. We expect peers to tell us when we are wrong." (Useful, for example, when an all-hands session's Q&A part is filled with crickets.)
- "That was the general plan. Now let us start the hole-poking session. Which part do you find most likely to fail?"

The language in all of these phrases is aimed at getting responses that are meatier than general nods of approval.

Embrace Feedback

Going hand in hand with giving permission and asking people to speak up is how you react when they finally do. I hope you know better than to shoot the messenger when someone tells you something that is not fun to hear, but the proper replies can help keep the flywheel going and encourage more feedback. First, people have to feel like they are being *listened to*. Whenever someone makes an effort to speak up and share their concerns or suggestions, it is not enough to merely nod and continue, even if you do not immediately find the input worthwhile.

Managers and especially high-level leaders should ensure that they understand what the feedback is about before addressing it. Asking clarifying questions and repeating what you heard in your own words helps validate that there are no misunderstandings and shows the other party that you are listening intently and taking the time to consider their suggestions. Without that, no matter how nicely you nod and smile, they are not likely to give it another shot.

Second, every piece of feedback should be leveraged, especially if it comes from a team that is usually less vocal. For example, when someone speaks up during an all-hands session, complimenting them for a well thought out suggestion or a question that is insightful in front of the team is essentially the opposite of shooting the messenger (hugging them?). Sharing during an update how someone spotted an issue with the current plan or came up with an improvement helps put those who speak up on a pedestal. It might feel a bit weird the first few times, but those are precisely the times that provide the most value in turning the ship around and starting to make feedback a regular occurrence in meetings.

Create Safety

The previous steps are all helpful in cultivating more psychological safety. However, some steps can be taken to address it directly. As much as managers are essential in responding to feedback, they have an equally important role in setting the correct standards between team members. I have seen cases in the past where teams had a clear divide: some felt absolute safety while others felt none.

Sometimes, it could be traced to issues of diversity and inclusion, but that is not always the case. There are enough "brilliant jerks" that are getting away with bulldozing and bullying others. A very clear bar of civility is required throughout your company. When someone regularly raises their voice and bangs on tables in discussions in a way that makes others uncomfortable, no psychological safety can prosper.

It is important to make everyone in your manager team realize the importance of modeling the civility bar. For example, say an incident similar to that described happens, and someone kept slamming on the desk out of anger. If no manager was present but heard about it later, what did they do? I have seen managers that completely ignored it (e.g., because this was one of their "star" coders), but let us assume they talked to the offending party one-on-one. The problem is that when no one else on the team knows that the issue has been handled, it is understood that these acts are condoned. Safety will be present only if the right atmosphere is meticulously upheld. It can take months to create, and a single offending incident suffices to reset all your efforts.

Diagnose Awkward Silences

Sometimes, your starting point is one where you have abundant examples of a lack of audacity and very little to go with when it comes to encouraging the existing bright spots. Do not let those failures, even small ones, go wasted. Your management team should be determined to squeeze whatever learning is possible from those incidents. At first glance, that might seem downright impossible. How can you leverage a lack of something? Luckily, we are not talking about alchemy and creating matter out of thin air. Once the paradigm shifts "click," you will find opportunities for growth everywhere.

One such example is to spot when the dogs fail to bark.[2] If you find out too late that some were aware of a problem but remained silent, dig into that. What was preventing them from speaking up and ringing the alarms? Depending on the situation and the personalities involved, sometimes this can be done in a postmortem meeting, and other times a one-on-one meeting will work better. I have had success in getting to the root of the inhibition to take in real-time by having these discussions done by a third party, such as an HR person. After all, if employees do not speak up due to a lack of psychological safety with their boss, they are not likely to tell that to their boss.

Another angle for maximizing your learning is to make the most out of staffing and management failures. Say that an employee has decided to leave the company. I recommend always having part of the exit interview revolve around these cultural issues. It might be even better to hold the exit interview or a follow-up a month or two after the employee has left. You would be surprised how much more willing to share candid feedback people become once they have decided to leave. Therefore, while you have lost that employee, you might learn something to prevent the next one from leaving.

BALANCING INTERNATIONAL DIFFERENCES

Special effort should be given to cultivating chutzpah in international organizations. As discussed previously, remote teams have a lot of advantages, but unlocking those requires intently "jelling" the different parts of the organization. Creating highly effective and candid remote teams can be challenging, but luckily some tactics can help you achieve that.

Mix It Up

The instinctive organizational topography when there are several sites is to create boundaries precisely around the team member's geographic location. Doing that often makes things easier in the short term but at the expense of collaboration and cross-organizational impact as time goes by. When we have geographically centered teams within an international company, we quickly see silos form and cultural differences fortify. You can tell that is happening when you hear people regularly reference them as "the X team," where you can replace X with a geographic identifier (e.g., the London team or the Polish team).

A counterintuitive approach that I have seen help induce healthier communication is to do the exact opposite. Aim to have teams that are small melting pots. Whenever possible, this tends to improve collaboration and enable more chutzpah immediately. The daily "friction" between the different cultures makes people adapt and learn faster. Further, you are leveraging your organization's diversity by having several people of different backgrounds and perspectives tackle each problem.

Just as cross-functional teams tend to work better when it comes to innovation and product mastery, so do cross-border teams and for similar motives. Encouraging R&D to go in this route, which has a longer ramp-up time for productivity than the alternative, can pay off as your company scales.

Rubbing Elbows

There are teams where individual contributors work by themselves and collaboration is kept to a minimum, and there are those teams that genuinely form a force multiplier effect where every member helps the rest. Many leaders default to the former way of operating because, on the surface, it has better throughput. If you have X engineers in the team, they can be working on X different tasks concurrently! However, that means that the employees do not get to collaborate enough on mundane day-to-day tasks. Those tasks are where the best work relationships are forged. When they work together mostly on contentious tasks or high-profile issues, it is often too late to create the rapport needed to foster chutzpah.

When people are colocated, it is more natural that they will work together on tasks spontaneously, but that is much harder for remote teams. To overcome it, leadership should invest in creating an environment that encourages such collaboration. One example is having the team come together for an offsite, as mentioned in Chapter 5. Do note that these cannot just be high-level planning offsite. If you manage to have the team work together physically for a week a year, you will reap the benefits for many months.

The rest of the time, invest in making collaboration happen regardless of location. That includes not demanding, as an executive team, that R&D prioritize throughput over other needs. It also means providing the budget for ensuring all parties have the equipment needed to collaborate effectively, like good microphones, a high-speed internet connection, and maybe even VR headsets.

Create Bridges

Lastly, you should accept the fact that cultural differences exist and find ways that make things easier and, with time, bring the different sides closer. One way is to invest in getting educated about the different cultures in the company. For example, it is prevalent in international corporations for everyone to know how "the Americans" work, be aware of their holidays, and work around their work hours. Real teams view everyone as peers, and therefore the effort should be mutual. I find that it is also part of the fascination with working in multinational companies.

Further, ensure that your hiring processes keep these cultural gaps in mind and screen for people that will work to bring people closer as opposed to deepening the chasm. You want people who are happy to collaborate with their remote peers and not get all grumpy because they need to start a video call to talk to them. Find employees who are open-minded and inclusive. Provide language lessons if necessary to lessen the language barrier.

Another small tactic is to try and hire immigrants and ex-pats in all locations. It might be harder to find these "unicorns." Still, it is invaluable in giving teams a quick boost in collaboration and understanding as long as they do not become the unofficial points of contact with the other team.

ACTION ITEMS

More *chutzpah* can give your company that extra *oomph* that it needs to save precious time and come up with more innovative ideas. You can start cultivating it today. Doing so throughout the company and not just in R&D will earn you extra credit.

- Take time to consider recent gaps of chutzpah.
- Assess what the hinderers of chutzpah in your organization are.
- Discuss what healthy audacity looks like and help your managers set the right expectations with their teams.
- Set an action plan to increase psychological safety.
- Give people permission to speak up and to fail.
- Diagnose the recent awkward silences.

NOTES

1. See Project Aristotle. https://rework.withgoogle.com/print/guides/5721312655835136/.
2. Sherlock Holmes realized in one of his cases that the dog did not bark at night while the incident was taking place, and therefore deduced the person was not a stranger to the dog. See https://en.wikipedia.org/wiki/The_Adventure_of_Silver_Blaze.

9

Debugging and Troubleshooting: What to Do When Things Don't Go According to Plans

No matter how well your R&D team is running, some problems are bound to happen. Especially for executives without a technical background, these issues might pose an incomprehensible obstacle. That is because they cannot be sure whether it is a genuine problem or whether the suggested solution is the right one.

In this chapter, I address the most common issues. Obviously, every case is different, so general advice might not fit your situation. Nevertheless, I intend to provide the same rules of thumb and direction I regularly give executives the first time we talk. That should help you decide on the right path forward faster. You can refer to the specific problems you will be tackling as you go along, but skimming it now might help you become aware of areas that require your attention.

PRODUCTIVITY PROBLEMS

The Team Seems to Be Going Slow Even though It Took on More People

I decided to open with this problem because it is one of the most common reasons I hear from companies and even from tech executives themselves. They often cannot put their finger on the cause and do not know what to do to correct things. All they can do is say that the pace seems too slow.

DOI: 10.4324/9781003358473-9

There might be a lot of reasons here, so it is best to start with a quick diagnosis. Was the team always slow and remained slow as it grew, or was it performing better? In the former case, it just might be that your expectations are not aligned with how long work actually takes. However, if this is not your first rodeo or other senior tech people voice this concern, you might have a deeper issue.

When this happens, I often suggest performing a survey to see what the team *is* doing, where their time is going, and to realize if there are other inhibiting factors. For example, there might be too many meetings, and a revamp of your processes is in order. Or they might be bogged down by quality issues, yet no time is ever spent on treating the root causes. If they keep focusing on the symptoms, the problems are bound to repeat.

In case of deterioration from a previous standard as the team grew, be aware that it is almost always the case in the first few months after teams grow. The extra effort necessary to bring the other engineers up to speed often takes a toll on the more experienced team members. Therefore your star engineers have less time to deliver themselves. This is known as Brooks's law:[1] adding people to a project that is behind schedule delays its completion even further. Things should get back to where they were and even improve within a quarter or two in case the team is not going through constant rapid hiring.

If enough time has passed and the unsatisfactory situation remains, it might be that the current organizational structure no longer fits the team's needs. For example, you might need to put in place additional or better tech leaders.

Are These Time Estimates Justified?

Like slow execution, many initiatives never even leave the drawing board because of hefty price tags. Executives are frustrated when they get idea after idea shut down with effort estimates that take considerably more than the leadership team was willing to spend on the feature or project. Often, these estimates are provided without any breakdown of the issues. I have seen CEOs demanding line item transparency for each part of an estimate to understand where the issue is. The problem is that this approach rarely solves the problem.

First, sometimes estimates are too long because the team bakes safety buffers into them. If they feel like they have to supply a date with 99%

certainty that the project will be done by then, it will be later off in the future compared to an estimate with 80% certainty. Being clear about how rigid the deadline is and how much wiggle room there will be for pushing it by a bit is critical to get honest estimates and reducing the fear of missing noncritical deadlines.

Second, if these estimates tend to be a take-it-or-leave-it sort of situation, you need to work on transforming it into a discussion and a collaboration opportunity. Providing atomic estimates without any flexibility or back and forth is how we work with vendors that we do not trust and the complete opposite of what an integrated and high-impact tech team should do. Teams should have enough safety, chutzpah, and product mastery to dig into the needs and better define the scope of the work.

For example, you want to hear replies like,

> Do we really have to support all geographies from the start? If we can focus just on these two markets for the first quarter, which are our natural starting points anyway, we can push off some regulatory needs and thus have our offering meet the market sooner.

That is how peers discuss and negotiate in order to achieve a win-win situation. Contrast that with an adversarial approach many teams seem to have.

Why Does It Seem Like We Cannot Improve Quality Issues?

If you are in this situation, you are suffering from having to repeatedly apologize to your customers about bugs, outages, and a lousy experience. Whenever that happens, the team (hopefully) drops whatever it is doing to solve the current issue and put out the fire, but the next problem will occur in a couple of days, like clockwork. Your customers' trust in the product is slowly abrading, and the tech team might be burning out from the constant rush to fix urgent problems.

To treat this scenario properly, the organization has to invest in diagnosis to get to the bottom of the issues and find the root causes. Otherwise, every emergency is like trying to put more duct tape on the product to make it hold up a bit longer; eventually, the whole thing is going to come down in shambles. Funny enough, sometimes teams need to be given permission the address problems thoroughly. Many, especially during crunch times, assume there is no time to do things properly and aim to sweep the issue under the rug as quickly as possible.

Deciding to allocate a portion of your team to tackle this also signals to everyone around how much the company values its quality, which can aid in ensuring that no new problems will be created while you work to fix the current ones. However, this is only a short-term solution. There needs to be a thorough postmortem that reviews the team's culture and practices that allowed things to get to this spot in the first place. Otherwise, you are doomed to end up in the same place sooner or later.

―――――

TECHNICAL ABILITY

Why Do They Keep Allocating Significant Time for This "Tech Debt"?

I have seen teams that go as far as allocating a third of their time to tech debt or "engineering needs" as part of their everyday processes. For others, this focus on tech debt manifests as a repeating request for yet another refactoring project. These take up a significant portion of the team's time, and sometimes no matter how much time they get, they still claim tech debt as the reason some new feature is impossible or would take a long time. The bottom line is that it feels like the team is treading water on this front. It is a never-ending journey.

As previously explained, there is nothing inherently wrong about teams that want to ensure the quality of their product, and everyone has to invest in keeping-the-lights-on work from time to time. The first typical reason for this focus tends to be that the team is too disconnected from product impact and therefore is drawn to fulfilling itself via tech mastery. If that is the case, I commend you to Chapter 6, where we covered this exact phenomenon. Remember that it is almost impossible to fix this if your tech executives are not aligned with the need for product mastery and possess it themselves. Therefore, sometimes the needed intervention is to help them before trying to get the rest of the team on board.

The second reason for this disconnect from product focus is that there are too many junior engineers, or at least a general lack of seniority, which often comes with a viewpoint that is too dogmatic. When they view things in black and white, any piece of code that is not up to the latest standards becomes an eyesore. Senior engineers tend to view these in gray scale and pick their fights. If this is the case, you can usually tell because the problem does not manifest at the same intensity throughout the organization. There will be bright posts that perform better. Leverage them by putting them on a pedestal or ask them to be more involved in other parts of the organization so their better traits will be copied.

Tech Is the Bottleneck for Our Business; Why Can't They Deliver?

Are you in a position where interested prospects are just waiting to use your product but cannot do so due to current product limitations? For example, are they waiting for a new integration to be created or for the technology to support a bigger scale needed to handle this new surge of clients? You are not alone. Sometimes, the business part seems to go smoothly, and I've seen plenty of CEOs very frustrated that they have "solved" the business part yet are restricted merely because of "slow coding."

First, I will place a disclaimer. It just might be that what you want the team to accomplish requires many iterations and a novel approach; therefore, it will take considerable time. For example, if you need a never-done-before artificial intelligence model that replaces what is currently only done by humans and at an extremely high level of accuracy, it might take years. Understand whether your bottlenecks are in areas that concern groundbreaking work or the more regular software engineering efforts that any other similar startup in your street is doing.

Assuming that the problems generally arise not just in your deep tech moats, then experience shows there are four leading causes. Some combination of these is likely the culprit, and you will have to diagnose it quickly to decide how to tackle the issue.

Lack of workforce: Addressed thoroughly below, sometimes it really is the case that the work to be done is simply too much for your existing team to achieve within the needed time frames.

Standards misalignment: When the executive team or product people come up with a roadmap and get in response a significant cost estimate without any back-and-forth, your tech team might be operating in order-taking mode. When this happens, it is very common that they understand some of the features and requirements as being significantly more elaborate and at a higher standard than is necessary at a given point.

For example, when you are just starting out with testing a new offering for a new market, you might have a roadmap item that says dashboards are required. The team might see that and have in mind a complete dashboard solution with customization, high-scale capabilities, and maybe even integrations with third parties. However, given the early stage, your product people might have merely put that there with the intent to have nothing more than two basic graphs at the beginning. Standards must be aligned to ensure that no extra effort goes into the product.

Poor clarity: Especially if your team was not being managed optimally prior, it is commonplace for R&D organizations to get bogged down with low-quality code that makes their work incredibly cumbersome and needlessly slow. This is what the infamous "tech debt" is all about. The team should not be given carte blanche to tackle quality indefinitely.

Instead, a clear plan that outlines the areas most harmful to productivity at the moment and the gains to be made by addressing them should be approved. This ensures a focus on addressing the problematic code from the viewpoint of getting back to impact. Further, an investigation or postmortem might be needed in order to find the root causes that have allowed the quality to deteriorate so much, or you will be in the same spot in a few months. Do keep in mind that it is the "easy route" for many engineers to silently accept tight deadlines and write subpar code that will weigh them down later, sometimes within days. Be mindful of using the urgency lever and urge them to speak up about issues.

Inexperience: Lastly, sometimes the team is plainly not experienced enough to achieve the goals in the needed time frame and costs. It might be that you need engineers with a specific specialty as you have embarked on a new direction or that you have to invest more in getting senior talent as opposed to people fresh out of college. Having a handful of engineers that have been through similar growing pains in other companies before can be invaluable for gaining momentum in tough times.

Of course, the issue might also be related to the experience of your tech leadership. Are they hiring the wrong people? Have they failed to create a focused culture with high product mastery? Suppose the tech executives and their engineering managers are not sufficiently connected to the business side or do not know how to cultivate a winning culture properly. In that case, you might have to inject experience one way or another (e.g., hire some experienced managers, invest in training, and get external advisory help and coaching).

Do We Really Need to Hire More People?

If your tech leaders or even the engineers themselves are coming up and saying that they are understaffed and ask for more budget to make the team larger, how can you tell whether this request makes sense? There are several ways to consider such an issue, even if you do not possess the expertise needed to plan an R&D team's work plan.

First, as we already covered in the first chapter, just because tech might seem more complicated or "scary" does not mean that it should be treated differently than other departments. I assume similar requests come up from sales departments and marketing organizations. If you have heuristics that work well there, try and apply the same logic. I state this first precisely to make you more comfortable using your leadership instincts the way you would with other disciplines in the company.

Next, there is an area where such requests are relatively easier to judge, and that is when the company is going through growth and expansion. When your product engineering organization has to keep doing what it has been doing while supporting an expansion to a new market or creating a new type of offering, it makes sense that some growth would be required. These scenarios might also arise when the tech team takes the initiative and makes the case to seize a new opportunity.

Things are not as straightforward when the team asks for more personnel simply to keep doing what it has been doing. Sometimes, even if you are not expanding the types of offerings, even honing your existing product creates more depth, similar to the growth described above. That is when hiring more might make sense. However, be very weary when staffing comes up as a solution for quality or delivery problems, especially if those are deviations from what the group was able to do prior. Throwing more people at the problem is, at best, an expensive Band-Aid.

TEAM HEALTH

Why Is Turnover High?

For engineering teams, a high employee churn rate can be crippling. Given the learning curve required to become proficient in a new environment, replacing any single effective individual contributor that leaves unannounced takes, on average, between three and six months. That is even harder when those employees have leadership positions. If your R&D team is suffering from a high turnover rate, it is vital to stop it before things spiral out of control.

First, are things considerably worse for R&D, or is your entire company suffering? It is natural for turnover in R&D to be slightly higher when compared to other departments because of a couple of factors. One is that talented engineers are always in demand and tend to switch jobs more easily. The other is that many bright engineers that remain on the bleeding edge of their industry are used to working on whatever is currently the shiny thing. Thus, make sure that the turnover is genuinely different from the rest of the company. If the problem is company-wide, you have bigger fish to fry.

Second, when engineers start to leave, it is crucial to understand the reason. Having exit interviews can be invaluable in surfacing issues. For example, I have seen cases where several engineers left and, in exit interviews, reported that the executive team was adamant about not listening to criticism from R&D regarding a certain issue. In reality, the problem boiled down to the CTO not doing his job properly when it came to bridging the gap between the two sides—the rest of the executives were oblivious to this being such a contentious problem.

There is no denying that at periods when the talent market is "hot," companies have to invest in retaining their top people. Suppose you are not offering salaries and perks comparable to other companies your size or, depending on your talent needs, even competitive. In that case, you will have a challenge reducing turnover. Similarly, it is hard to bring in people when your tech stack is outdated and is no longer "sexy" enough.

As tough as it is to admit it, sometimes companies end up with solutions that are no longer considered viable in the long term (unfortunately, given the rapid pace at which things change, I have seen this happen to companies with products that were less than a year or two old). When this happens, engineers might feel the need to jump ship in order to ensure that they remain "hirable." They might feel it is too risky for their career to work on technology considered outdated for too long. If this is the case, your tech executives should devise a plan for incrementally modernizing your product. Keep in mind that obsolete technologies also tend to be more neglected and thus get technological innovations later and are more prone to bugs and cyber vulnerabilities.

We Cannot Seem to Hire People

Often going hand in hand with high turnover is the inability to fill open positions. It is not uncommon to see companies that claim to be trying to staff the same position for six months, unsuccessfully. Your tech leaders might just shrug and blame it on the market, but you should not let them off the hook that easily.

While there is no denying that, at times, it can be much harder to hire senior engineers, the reality is that essentially every time I saw a company bemoaning such a situation, I knew of another comparable company (sometimes literally in the same office building!) that was doing much better. Your tech leaders are a crucial part of attracting talented employees.

Your hiring process needs to be analyzed and sometimes overhauled. For example, in many tech hubs, you will have a much higher chance of landing top talent if your interviewing process is condensed to a single day instead of having three stages separated by days or weeks. You should also invest in training everyone involved in the hiring process to know how to sell the company to candidates.

Another facet of creating a company that is a talent attractor is to work on employer branding early on. This is a long-term effort, but it pays off. I bet that your sales and marketing people are regularly attending conferences and talking about your product. Something similar should be taking place at the technological level. The team should be "tooting its own horn" and letting it be known the type of excellent engineering that is taking place. By speaking at conferences, hosting meet-ups, and working in the open, they create a name for your company. That, when tailored properly, will help lure the types of candidates you are looking for.

Tech Leadership Is Not Taking the Lead

Sometimes, no matter how much autonomy and direction you provide, you might feel like your tech executives are simply not interested in being proactive. Perhaps you have read the previous parts of this book and thought to yourself that what I am talking about sounds nice but also delirious. The truth is that sometimes even talented and experienced tech executives might not be a good fit for *your* company right *now*.

Have an open discussion with them and provide clear and concise feedback: where are they lacking, what should they be doing differently, and how do you measure their success? Without being crystal clear, you will never be able to tell whether they understand your expectations. Do this with the timeline in mind. Progress should be visible almost immediately, and a positive trend should be clearly established within a couple of months. If things do not improve enough, you should consider an experience injection by bringing in external help or, perhaps, changing tech leadership.

Several times in the past, I could determine within a single meeting that things were not going to work out between a tech executive and the company. The reason is rarely that the person I was talking to was not adept or lacked skills. It almost always boils down to a cultural fit with the company and how the executive team operates. The relevant factors are how much autonomy the tech executive has and style preferences. For the former, consider adjusting accordingly for leaders that you trust. The latter really changes between companies and might indicate that you have a mismatch.

If you fear there's a mismatch, I will tell you my magic question—though I have to warn you that I find it often works better when asked by someone external like myself when working with clients. The question is,

> Say I could wave a magic wand, and tomorrow morning, you could be done with this role, just like that. No one is angry, and the company will magically make do without you. Would you ask me to use the wand or not?

You would be amazed how easy it is to tell that someone is going to eventually part ways by watching the duration of the silence after I ask this.

IMPACT

The Team Seems to Be Repeatedly Delivering the Wrong Things

When sprint after sprint (or even worse, quarter after quarter), the team's output is always off, you likely have a communication problem. This is the case when the team is not doing tech for tech's sake or focusing solely on tech debt. They are genuinely putting in the hours working toward product improvements. Yet it seems like there is a lot of failure work involved: after the first iteration, like clockwork, discrepancies are uncovered and more time needs to be spent to find a way to make what you have resemble what you actually need.

First, this might happen simply because the team is not utilizing enough chutzpah. Even when what is asked of them seems unclear, they try and plow ahead without asking clarifying questions or speaking up and saying that it does not make sense. Consider a quick chutzpah intervention to encourage everyone to speak sooner rather than later.

A second culprit might be a lack of ongoing collaboration between R&D, Product, and stakeholders. Even if everything seems crystal clear initially, things quickly get fogged up as progress is made. That is since every day of coding entails dozens of micro-decisions. If all of those are done without communication with those who understand the users best, you will see a slow drift from vision to implementation. We stressed the importance of product mastery to ensure that more of these micro-decisions are done correctly. Still, even the best organizations cannot entrust all of these decisions to R&D. Make all the relevant parties work side by side (e.g., in cross-functional squads) until you see an improvement.

One last aspect to consider is vision clarity. If you or the product team are not entirely clear on what needs to be done in the first place, how can you expect your engineers to be any better? If that is the case, any iteration and step forward are not solely about cranking about features but about gaining insights and learning more to decide about the next cycle. Therefore, be frank about the general lack of clarity and do not attempt to bolt down huge roadmaps ahead of time. Embrace the iterative process.

How Do You Handle Cases Where the Engineers Seem to Be Focused on the Wrong Things?

Unlike the previous problem, this situation is one where you can clearly tell that the team has not set its sights on the business objectives. Instead, they might push for more tech debt time and refactoring.

If your tech leaders are backing these requests, you owe them to hear their case and not dismiss it immediately. However, their side of the deal is that they have to make a business case for this work. When the requests are not automatically rejected or accepted, both sides better understand the other's needs. When you reach a decision to delay an infrastructure project or minimize its scope, your tech leaders will be able to explain this to the team when you have arrived at a decision after a discussion.

However, when individual contributors and team leaders request these initiatives, but your senior staff seem to oppose them as well, then you might have a problem in getting people's buy-in to your business objectives and product priorities. Frequently this is because not enough effort is made to communicate these aspects to those in the company's trenches. As we discussed when covering motivational pulls, every highly effective team is one where the business side is made comprehensible enough to draw people's attention more than the shiny tech side.

They Don't Seem to Really Be Working Hard

This is a problem that I sometimes get asked only between meetings and in a hushed voice. No one likes feeling like they are a micromanager or one of those stereotypical TV bosses from hell. However, just because executives do not ask these questions aloud to their team does not mean they don't *think* about it. Regarding how the work of R&D teams looks, there are two crucial things to learn.

The first part is that software engineering is knowledge work and is not merely a matter of how quickly people punch in code. Someone taking half an hour to ponder something might save days of work. You shouldn't look at how long people sit at their desks (well, if you have a hybrid workplace, you cannot do that even if you wanted to). Engineering productivity is more complicated than that. As a freelancer, I would accomplish more in two days a week than most engineers around me did in a whole week (those are the words of my clients). That is not because I was typing super hard all day long. I was simply highly attentive to impact and focus, and thus delivered the most impactful and client-centered output I could every week. So however you are used to measuring other employees, with engineering it makes less sense to look at the input to assess their productivity.

The second bit is about how *should* productive teams look. You cannot judge it by their input, as we just said. What remains is the outcome of their efforts. Is the team achieving results in a timely manner? After all, you are not interested in how long it takes them to write the code. I assume you'd happily double salaries if they could deliver the work within a day whenever a new iteration starts. Thus, providing the team with business objectives and seeing their progress toward them helps assess whether the team is working properly.

However, two caveats are always hard to tackle. The general velocity of the team is hard to measure objectively. Assuming that the team is delivering whatever business objectives they committed to in the quarter, how can you tell they shouldn't have done even more? Some proxy indicators might help, like comparing the different teams in a group or getting an external opinion.

Similarly, when you work at a resolution of teams and their objectives, it is harder to spot star players and people that are not carrying their own weight. My usual advice is to trust your tech leaders to be in charge of this level of management, given that they and their management teams are more involved. Nevertheless, there is a wave of new startups aimed at making engineering productivity more transparent and measurable at all levels of the R&D organization. Having seen some of these at their current stages, I predict it will be easier to gain semi-objective assessment within a few years.

How Hands-On Should My Tech Executive Be?

It might be that you are hiring a tech executive or looking at how those you already have are operating and wondering whether they should be more in the trenches. For example, I know CEOs who found it odd that their VP of Engineering did not know what each engineer in the team was doing, even at large organizations.

My general rule of thumb for early-stage organizations is that tech leaders should have enough hands-on knowledge to help and guide the work. Otherwise, they might struggle to manage their team and build an organization that does not need them for handholding as it grows. The larger and more mature the company is, the less hands-on all of your tech leaders need to be. For example, a VP of R&D in charge of a hundred people often has not written code for a few years, but the CTO or Chief Architect might still be writing code regularly.

Do note that even leaders with hands-on knowledge do not necessarily need to use that ability. I know tech leaders that worked hard to remain hands-on even as their teams grew and others that couldn't wait for the organization to grow enough so they would not need to do just that. This is a matter of managerial style. I believe that if the leader is on top of everything, they should be able to go either way. If you feel like one way or another is critical for how your company runs, it should be discussed as part of assessing cultural fit.

ACTION ITEMS

This is a different type of chapter; therefore, we will not list action items. The essential takeaway is to see how many problems or issues you are seeing frequently. Many more problems are common, but there are only so many pages we can devote to these. You can find an archive of articles on typical issues along with new content regularly on my website.[2] You don't have to go it alone.

NOTES

1. Coined by Fred Brooks. See https://en.wikipedia.org/wiki/Brooks%27s_law.
2. See https://avivbenyosef.com.

10

Crypto, NFTs, and Metaverses, Oh My!: Handling Hype and Trends

Earlier in my career, I was one of the best-known global experts in a framework for writing websites that was, at the time, the fastest-growing tool. I spoke at conferences, was flown to deliver training, wrote a book, and had millions of visits to my website. That was the case during 3–4 years, and then it went the way of any popular piece of tech and started diminishing in stature. Within a couple of years, it was already considered "legacy" and is, by now, no longer really used for anything new. *Sic transit gloria mundi.*

That specific experience taught me it is futile to rely on any particular piece of technology as a silver bullet. Everything eventually changes. This is a double-edged sword: what makes technology such a force to be reckoned with—the rapid pace at which it evolves and becomes better—makes it so that no one can sit still for too long. Many leaders understand this issue, but their approach to handling it is unproductive. Having a system to help you address the many changes technology will go through is incredibly useful in helping your team stay on track.

Note: The technologies listed in the title of this chapter are all chosen to be examples of trendy buzzwords at the time of this writing that many do not really grok. At the risk of timing this chapter, I decided to pick them to help induce the uneasiness many experience when technologies they do not understand are discussed. These specific choices are not material, and a few years ago, they could have just as easily been replaced with big data, cloud, machine learning, mobile, and many more.

DOI: 10.4324/9781003358473-10

TECH VERTIGO

Many software engineers lament how tough it is to remain up-to-date given the fast-moving nature of the industry. Therefore, it is undoubtedly an even greater problem for those removed from the work and yet need to remain current with changes that can affect their company's strategy. While there are different ways companies try to handle this, there are two most common scenarios.

The first is the ostrich method, where the company seems to stick its head in the sand and ignore any changes in the landscape until they have no other option. While this is successful in avoiding the dizziness that comes with alternating between technologies every other week, it means that you are becoming vulnerable to disruption by those on the bleeding edge. I do not believe this extreme is viable for anyone who intends to embrace technology fully.

The contrasting option is the capricious team that seems to change tech plans as part of the weekly planning effort. These companies have succumbed to FOMO[1] or external factors of little importance, such as appearing trendy. Regardless of whether these haphazard changes are done by the urging of the tech people or higher up, the result is the same: technology for technology's sake. You might gain a nice mention in the media but at the price of retaining a focused effort on impact.

THE IOS FEATURE RUSH

To make the previous scenario more vivid, let us consider something that I have seen happen at many companies every year: companies scrambling to make use of new iOS capabilities in the run-up to the major yearly release. Apple announces a new version of its operating system for iPhones every June, which tend to become globally available in September, along with the release of a new generation of phones. Apps that use the newly announced features on the day of the release have a higher chance of being featured by Apple.

When those new capabilities happen to coincide with features that match the company's vision or that would provide customers with value, that is great. What you get is a win-win situation. However,

I have often seen companies bent over backward to try and find a justification to implement a feature that simply had no real merit. Countless companies have routinely lost a quarter of development in the hopes of being featured for a few days. I do not believe that the users who get those apps in search of new capabilities and see that they don't really make sense are likely to become fans of the product. Do you?

I was once on a team that did precisely this. We got nice media coverage, the engineers felt "cool" for doing something trendy, and the company got a small wave of new users. Fast-forward a couple of weeks, those users were gone, the media had moved on, and we were stuck with supporting a feature that provided little material benefit.

You cannot always aim to make use of the latest and greatest. You had lost that battle even before the first shot was fired. It induces cultures that tread water for months instead of making steady progress forward, and the harm to focus outweighs the benefits. Instead, you must strike a healthy balance and avoid spinning your wheels.

REPLACING FRIVOLITY WITH CALCULATED BETS

Effective tech leadership requires finding an equilibrium that ensures your team remains abreast of technological advancements and improvements to exploit them when they make sense without getting into vertigo. It is easier said than done, but the executive team can help find such a balance by setting up the appropriate culture.

Treating Fads as Fads

When the company's management and product leaders suffer from FOMO, fads seem to find their way to product roadmaps. Just because your friends are struggling to fit a round blockchain peg in the square hole that is their offering does not mean that you have to do the same. In the example of the iOS feature rush above, leadership should learn to weigh the tangible benefit these dashes provide and only ask the team to do it if it makes sense.

If you avoid this discipline, your tech team will likely be unproductive in the short and long term. First, when these sprints to get something out the door fast are performed is often when a piece of technology is still immature and therefore tends to have a lot of limitations and bugs as well as a lack of experts. Thus, making use of a new iOS capability is always more time-consuming the first month than it is a quarter later after many bugs have been fixed and online resources and guides have been created. Sometimes, waiting a bit can save a lot of effort and provide your users with a better result right from the start.

Second, the predisposition to change plans regularly to perform work that has little impact or a strategic justification chafes away the team's confidence in the company's direction. When they work hard to get a new feature ready at arbitrary deadlines (e.g., whenever Apple decides to release its new phones) and see that those features are forgotten a couple of weeks later, they are less likely to work hard the next time an opportunity presents itself—even if that might be one that genuinely matters.

However, I do not expect your leaders to be purists. Sometimes companies invest in something because it looks good in the news cycle or helps with the brand image. If that is the case, it should be candidly treated as such. The requirements and need definitions should all take that context into consideration, which would then, for example, allow the team to invest less in details that do not matter. That way, at least no one feels like they wasted their time implementing a state-of-the-art capability only for it to be abandoned in days.

Keeping a Finger on the Pulse

To avoid the ostrich method, the company should have a mechanism to evaluate new advancements and test them before committing to them. This ongoing openness to innovation and trying out new tools is part of the culture described in Chapter 6. By deciding as a company to make room for creativity and experiments, you can shape the way trends are viewed by everyone. Instead of making people feel like they have to fight to check anything new or work long hours, you can make intermissions regularly scheduled.

When the team knows that the next innovation sprint is around the corner, employees are more likely to keep track of these ideas and pull them out in time for the intermission. That allows them to entirely focus on their work the rest of the time with the confidence that nothing major will be left aside for too long. Then, your brightest people will tinker and play with whatever they have collected since the last intermission. Some of these experiments will quickly make it clear that your company can put something aside for the time being (yes, it probably makes little sense to replace your in-app chat with a blockchain-based solution).

But, every couple of intermissions, experiments might uncover a promising prospect. Armed with a proof-of-value from the intermission, the team can promote those experiments with the most encouraging results.

Demanding Business Cases

Armed with those ideas that have gone through basic validation as part of an intermission or other exploration time, the company's leadership should make a deliberate decision about whether to go forward with it and how. As opposed to rushing with something that seems cool but does not necessarily align with the current roadmap, these decisions should consider the novelty of the approach as a single facet of it and not focus solely on it.

To do so, those championing this specific technology should make a business case for it. I have seen countless startups where the tech people had a unique and novel technological solution—but no problem accompanying it. To be sure that this is not such a case, a clear business case for using this technology, or at least a hypothesis that makes sense, should be clearly articulated. Changes to the current roadmap should only be done when the potential reward justifies the disruption to work and the risks involved.

No matter what change you are looking at, consideration should be given to the following:

- Opportunity cost: What would you be giving up to prioritize this change?

- Immaturity: As already described, there is increased complexity when using technology before it matures since it is likely to be less stable and fewer helpful resources are available.
- Maintenance: Code always has some maintenance involved, and bleeding-edge solutions tend to require more maintenance. That is because if the technology is still evolving rapidly, an effort is needed to bring it up to date.
- Half-life time: Is this solution something that has the potential to genuinely improve your product in the long term? Is it solely a fad and likely to no longer provide any edge in a month or two after everyone else has added it or has forgotten about it?

Note that this discussion relates to technological changes that affect the product's behavior or roadmap timeline. For these, a good rule of thumb is that if the idea is promising enough, a stakeholder or product leader should also believe in it. Any internal changes should be left to the R&D team's consideration. For example, replacing some internal tool for another should not require outside approval if it can be done for a relatively low cost along with the rest of the team's work. In Figure 10.1, you can see the funnel-like process that you should put in place.

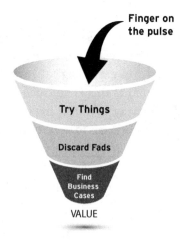

FIGURE 10.1
The valuable tech initiatives funnel.

GOT TALENT

There is no denying that your engineering group will need to play around with new technologies from time to time to remain current. However, not every engineer can effectively play around with any new piece of technology. Sometimes, the trend *du jour* might be something your team simply does not comprehend. Understanding how your tech talent composition plays into leveraging advancements is crucial for creating the right type of innovative team.

Tailoring Experiments to Your Team

It is much easier to consider your team's current strengths and advantages and ensure that you get a reliable lead in those areas. For example, I've worked with companies that develop products for software engineers, who, on average, tend to use the latest software and be early adopters. One such company had a team that was already very attuned to trends in the software development world simply because that was where their passion lay.

Making the most of their strength, that team was always among the first in the world to tinker with a new framework or integrate with a new service once it seemed to attract any attention. Since they were already glued to Product Hunt[2] and the likes, it was easy for them to spot opportunities. Attempting to create such an atmosphere without a team already drawn to this world would have been considerably harder (yet possible).

Sometimes, it is not straightforward to determine which areas the team has an advantage in and that also align with the company's products. When the stakeholders shoot down this approach in general, you might hinder innovation that you could benefit from at virtually no cost, especially in cases like the above, where the team is likely to be tinkering and staying up to date regardless. Encouraging this sort of trendiness also helps with morale and motivation. An executive team that allows this to happen without even allocating many resources for it specifically can reap many benefits.

Team Adjustment

Sometimes, the team's current proficiencies and areas of interest do not overlap enough with some of the possible sources for your next leap forward.

For example, over the past few years, several companies have realized that AI should constitute a larger part of their strategy. However, this field of software engineering is relatively new and is only now becoming more of a commodity. Therefore, the senior tech leadership saw the need to start experimenting with AI but had no one fit for the role.

When you spot such a clear gap, adjusting your team to have that talent will allow you to ensure you do not miss an opportunity (or become vulnerable to market disruption on that front). Depending on your needs, you can take a few approaches to perform this talent adjustment.

Get external experts: When the trend you want the team to experiment in still has significant risks associated with it, or is vague as opposed to a safe bet, then committing to having full-time employees work on it might not be the best choice. By relying on external experts, you can consult people who have already done similar projects in the past and have them kick off the first couple of experiments that are most appropriate for your situation. Freelancers and domain-specific consultants are pricier than most employees but can also provide a tremendous return on investment. They take less time to bring in (as they don't need to give any notice), they have a broad perspective, and they are flexible. If the direction turns out to be bad for the company, you can easily part ways with no strings attached.

Train in-house: Especially in cases where the technical domain you need a boost in is currently hyped and viewed as shiny and attractive, you might already have a bunch of engineers who understand your business and are motivated to learn this new domain. If you are pretty certain about the need, e.g., this is not a long shot, but in fact, a bet that seems pretty safe, then investing in having part of your in-house team gain competence can make sense. Do note that depending on the learning curve, this is not a rapid solution and might not be appropriate in case you need a novel approach. People just learning the technology might have too shallow an understanding to do things never done before.

Hire: This option should be kept for when your leadership team is confident that the technology you are considering will be useful for the company in the long term. When you know something is more than a mere fad, it can make sense to invest in hiring full-time employees to help push it forward. This is the middle-ground between the previous two options. Nevertheless, it involves filling new positions for this purpose and thus should be used when there is high certainty and a specialized area that requires deep expertise.

There are jack-of-all-trades engineers, and then there are specialist engineers. The former are sometimes referred to as "full stack engineers," while the latter are narrowly focused on a certain part of the tech stack. Full-stack engineers are often valuable force multipliers in teams. They are flexible and thus can work on different parts of the system depending on the company's current needs. They are also more autonomous, as they can take care of more features and tasks in a comprehensive end-to-end manner.

However, full stackers are not ideal for every role. They tend to go for breadth, but some areas benefit from depth and having a profound understanding of a particular field. When this is the case, you are probably better off hiring people with this specific orientation as opposed to letting your star full-stackers learn the ropes quickly. Especially when great novelty is needed, engineers with a shallow understanding are often capped and do not understand things deeply enough to tinker with them freely.

MOONSHOTS AND CUTTING-EDGE TECHNOLOGY

One interesting notion to keep in mind when considering technology that is still in its infancy is that it could be very hard even for experts to determine whether something will have a substantial impact on the industry or turn out to be a fad quickly to be forgotten. Sometimes, the line between the two is even harder to discern. For example, consider machine learning. For over a decade, the term was used by many startups eager to proclaim their superiority, where in fact, those in the know could tell how often the "machine learning" at play was essentially composed of basic rule-based logic and human help behind the scenes.

Thus, for those who could not quickly look at what a company was offering and determine the complexity of the solution, it might have seemed from the outside as if machine learning was being used everywhere and that it was rapidly developing. Since it was frequently boasted without merit, there were those software engineers that deemed the entire concept a fad. To an extent, they were right for many years. Nevertheless, there were always those who kept honing their genuine machine learning–based solutions. One such example is a client of mine where I witnessed how their solution was gradually becoming more innovative and efficient, reducing the overhead of human analysts by significant improvements with every year that passed.

That is why some of the newer public offerings in artificial intelligence caught so many by surprise. When "basic" machine learning was relatively rare, how could anyone expect anything remotely akin to intelligence to be anywhere near? When advancements in AI generating text and images started appearing in rapid succession, such as ChatGPT,[3] DALL·E 2,[4] and Stable Diffusion,[5] many were flabbergasted. Technology sometimes requires years of steady improvement to reach a point where it can be easily utilized for business. This raises a couple of questions. How can you ensure that your team will not get blindsided by such an improvement? And should your R&D group act as an industry-wide arrowhead for any such technological advancement?

Uncovering Blind Spots

Earlier, we discussed the importance of letting business cases direct the majority of tech exploration work. Given that teams can devote only so many hours to trying out new things and experimenting, it makes sense to ensure that most of these are calculated bets where you can demonstrably see the benefit to your product or customers. That is why there is a balancing act needed to keep in mind the trade-off between value-centered experiments and keeping your eye on developments that might turn into moonshots.

When discussing calculated bets, we always weigh the two parts of a gamble: the risk it entails and the potential upside. Figure 10.2 helps demonstrate the balancing of risk and reward. Moonshots are those bets with a small chance of success but a commensurately more significant benefit should they happen. How much larger changes with how high the stakes are, but a genuine moonshot is one where the possible windfall is an order of magnitude greater than the investment required. Your tech team should judiciously look for opportunities where these moonshots make sense.

However, no one should jump right into a moonshot that requires months of effort or considerable expense without due diligence. As part of intently uncovering blind spots, small experiments and bite-sized research tasks can be utilized. Doing so routinely and checking possible directions as those come up lowers the risks of large blind spots forming. Exploration will spot wherever a new technology is still too unstable, warrants deeper research, or is not relevant to your needs.

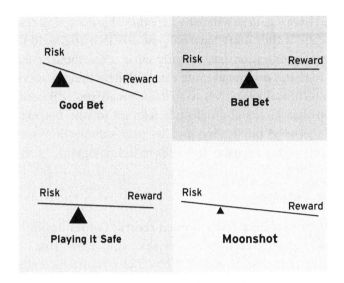

FIGURE 10.2
Different types of bets.

How can you know that R&D won't miss topics that should be checked? Ensure they do not become ensconced in their comfort zones and regularly look around. The basic precept is to help increase the "surface area" of R&D with the outside world, thus improving the odds that they stumble upon interesting ideas. A team with its head down cannot see anything new.

Consider the team's participation in the industry's largest conferences and technological exhibitions. These can vary wildly, but some examples include Apple's WWDC and Google's I/O for those developing on their platforms, Black Hat for cyber research, and CES for broad exposure. While it is usually impossible to send more than a handful of people to a conference, investing in training and workshops to help keep larger portions of the group up to date is also worthwhile.

Sometimes you can bring in global experts to work with the team closely, but that is not always possible. Lucky for us, there are sundry possibilities available. My favorite secret tactic for gaining exposure to promising technologies requires minimal investment but pays off considerably.

Whenever there are areas that I think one of my clients needs to pay specific attention to, we take the time to find a handful of the most prominent thought leaders about the subject and their online presence. Often, they will have a Twitter account that can be followed. That's an excellent first step. However, we dig a bit deeper. Frequently, one of those leaders will have a paid newsletter where they share ongoing research and developments. If they don't have one, use a search engine to find which newsletter or publication has recently cited these thought leaders and subscribe to that. I am mentioning this trick here because it is one I also advise nontechnical executives to follow, though you will need to find a publication that speaks at an altitude relevant to you. For example, the superb *Stratechery*[6] publication and its paid subscription are great for maintaining healthy exposure to trends in technology.

Tech for Tech's Sake

At the risk of sounding like a broken record, I'm reminding you once more that exploring tech for tech's sake might be "fun," but when that is the only incentive, it is a hobby, not a profitable endeavor. On the one hand, the executive team should give the team enough slack to tinker and poke around with ideas from time to time, even when those experiments might lead to a dead end. On the other hand, if this experimentation never results in praxis but is solely theoretical, the team will become accustomed to this and stop driving toward applying what they learn in real life.

To find the right balance, my recommendation is that you establish a measurement that will be used to keep everyone in line. For example, you can have a metric that says that at least one experiment every quarter should result in a traceable improvement in the product or that once a year, 5–10% of the company's new value or sales should rely on features that could not be offered before a certain leap was made. Even though these metrics can be somewhat tricky, or if the team fails to hit them all time, merely stating these goals and having them discussed means that those involved in the work will remember the end goal of their experiments and are thus more likely to succeed in finding applications for them.

ACTION ITEMS

You are now equipped to fight FOMO. Like a swift martial arts move, whenever that anxiety creeps up, you should find a way to leverage it as an opportunity to uncover new aspects of technology and remain current. Do this today:

- Stop any initiative you might have in progress that's simply rooted in fear or capriciousness.
- Assess the business case for each technological effort that is not directly connected to product improvements.
- Evaluate your existing talent and the areas where your technological edge lies and decide whether to double down on your strengths or inject external expertise.
- Ensure that your team is not afraid of giving moonshots a try every now and then. When was the last time? Discuss inhibitors.
- Establish a metric for keeping tech for tech's sake at bay.

NOTES

1. Fear of missing out.
2. A popular website for launching new products and startups. https://www.product-hunt.com/.
3. See https://openai.com/blog/chatgpt/.
4. See https://openai.com/dall-e-2/.
5. See https://stability.ai/.
6. See https://stratechery.com/stratechery-plus/.

11

Could You Tell if It Hit You in the Face?: Benchmarks for a Successful Tech Team

No company set out to hire a tech team because the executive team wanted to see pretty code. Alas, when leadership lacks other tools for measuring their tech efforts, the only way to justify ROI is to look at output, not outcomes. This makes teams myopic and reduces their leverage. The proper yardstick can unlock talent growth and help you keep the flywheel spinning. Just as you hold the sales team accountable to quotas and marketing to lead generation goals, so should you know what to expect from a profitable and innovative tech team.

MEASURING SUCCESSFUL TECH EXECUTIVES

Your input and influence on R&D start with the executives you put in place to lead it and how these executives are managed. We have all seen cases where a problematic executive hindered the progress of an otherwise excellent team. To avoid these scenarios and spot them when they occur, you should clearly define what success would look like for your different tech leaders.

Being Good Leaders

Sometimes, CEOs ask me how they can even tell whether their tech executives are doing well. When asked for their ideas, they merely shrug because they view technology as an eccentric creature that behaves

DOI: 10.4324/9781003358473-11

differently from the rest of the company. Other times, they think that their tech leaders should be treated differently because they are "geeks" and do not act like other executives in the company.

The truth is that tech executives are *executives* first and should therefore be measured like you would any other senior leader. Some of these aspects might be slightly adjusted for the technological world, but even then, they should be pretty familiar. Every executive's "output" is the organization they lead and its ability to get the work done. Therefore, before measuring the organization's results, consider whether the executive is performing well when it comes to creating the best possible team.

First, consider whether they seem capable of managing the current team and growing it to where it needs to get in the foreseeable future. Growing the team has two sides here. One is about the straightforward aspect of staffing the team to match growth plans. Too many executives consider hiring and staffing a chore, which is wrong. Hiring is, practically, the most important thing an executive is in charge of since it is the staff they bring on that will determine the quality of the work. Do you feel like your tech leaders are setting up hiring systems appropriate for the company's current stage? These systems usually need to be refreshed with every new "generation" of growth. Good executives address hiring with alacrity.

The other side of growth is about maximizing the potential of the people you already have. A healthy organization is one that is constantly evolving and becoming even better. Without that, groups devolve into the common trope of the company that only gets slower as it brings on more people. When teams evolve with a solid foundation, you tend to see some employees become more prominent and gain more leverage over the rest of the company. If the same small group of people is communicating with the rest of the company quarter after quarter, that can be an external indicator of talent stasis. Considering common team health measures such as turnover, time to staff open positions, and Peter Pan counts[1] is useful.

Second, your tech executives should perform well as executives in general. Consider these aspects:

Part of the executive team: The tech executives should not confine themselves to the technical corner of the company and shy away from the rest of the leadership work. Have they developed good working relationships with the other executives in the company? Can they communicate with them jargon-free and achieve conceptual agreement about substantial changes and roadmaps without the need for an intermediary?

Taking the initiative: This is a term I picked up from chess which relates to being the one currently on the offensive and making steps first, forcing the other side to become reactive. While chess is a zero-sum game, relationships within the company have a different nature, and it is possible to have multiple people taking the initiative concurrently. That is the difference between having to tell people what to do and having them come up to you with ideas and suggestions. What is the use of a highly paid VP if all they do is sit and wait for you to give them directions?

Moving upstream: Connecting the previous two points together, moving upstream is about executives who do not fear operating with a company-wide focus. They do not pigeonhole themselves to technical issues. For example, these executives find the time to talk to customers and attend board meetings. They do not view executive work as a necessary evil but as part of how they become even greater force multipliers. An executive that speaks up during strategy brainstorms or roadmap planning sessions is an executive that has a bigger impact on the company as well as is more involved and engaged. It is healthier for all involved.

Tech Leadership

Other than the general qualities that any good executive should possess, some skills can make a tech leader much more capable of running a top-percentile organization. These are the top four skills that I always keep in mind when coaching tech executives:

Clarifying vision: As the saying goes, no wind is a good wind when you do not know where you're headed. While tech organizations should not develop mountains of tech strategy documents, they need a clear vision of their path forward. What forms the basis of the company's technical competitive advantage? How does innovation play into the team's strengths? Which initiatives are required?

It is perfectly fine for a tech executive not to form the vision entirely alone. Sometimes your executives excel in running teams and are not necessarily the best experts you have with regard to specific technical areas. Nevertheless, a capable executive ensures the formation of such a vision and its subsequent championing. This vision serves a critical part in aligning the entire team's creativity along the axis of most impact.

Further, there comes a time for any organization when things are not performing optimally, and it can be easily seen that the team has diverged from its previous standards. Part of forming a cogent and actionable vision is about being able to spot these and articulating a way to address the issues. A CEO once told me how her R&D group had been underperforming for months. She tasked the three tech executives with coming up with a plan. Their suggested solution had nothing to do with the problems. They suggested forming guilds, which are technically oriented groups that are in charge of improving technical ability and quality, while the problem was that the teams were not working well together! If your leaders cannot suggest a path forward out of their currently problematic areas, how can you expect them ever to improve the state of their group?

Manifesting solutions: They should have an executive mindset, which is the mirror image of that veteran senior software engineer that has become cynical, pessimistic, and dry. The last thing a board needs when trying to come up with ways to propel the company forward is someone sitting there, repeatedly shooting down any idea and suggestion. Those with an executive mindset have two crucial skills. First, when they hear about needs and opportunities, they fight the urge to automatically spot all the possible issues and immediately pounce on the meat of the suggestion: what precisely makes this important, which aspects of the problem are genuinely constants, and which can be changed, why hasn't it been done already?

The second skill is instilling the same attitude in their teams. They are inured to skepticism and find a way to convey the same suspension of disbelief to the rest of the group. When people then consider things from that point of view that assumes a solution exists, they are doubly as likely to find that solution. Your tech executives should not act like bureaucrats that just tell you why things can't work.

Creating external value: Though this is not always the responsibility of tech executives, they frequently have to communicate with parties external to the company. For example, they might work with customers and prospects or help integrate with different partners.

This skill does not come easily to everyone, and you should evaluate whether you can trust them to manage such situations successfully. An executive that cannot be trusted to talk to a client alone is adding overhead.

Further, creating external value is about more than merely talking to people as part of their job. Since the most valuable asset any R&D group has is its talent pool, working on employee branding is highly important for growing teams. Similar to creating a vision, these leaders don't have to be those who do all the work themselves and might rely on engineers who enjoy giving talks or hire developer relations specialists. No matter *how* they do it, they are in charge of the *what*.

Culture forming: Lastly, since every executive's product is their organization, effectively shaping the organization's culture is crucial for success. Do you feel that your tech team views itself as an integral part of the rest of the company or tends to be aloof and disconnected from others? Do they embody the company's values? These things never come by without leaders who are *actively* helping mold the team.

As covered throughout this book, it takes two to tango. You cannot capitalize on tech's promise without giving it the autonomy it requires and without your tech team willing to improve and achieve dramatic results. The latter often starts with having tech leaders that help instill the needed vision and values into the team and guide their managers into forming an organization that prioritizes teamwork and cooperation above its own technical cleverness.

MEASURING TEAMS

Many CEOs have told me that, as outsiders, they find it incredibly difficult to tell whether their tech team is operating well. I disagree. I think they approached me precisely because they had a bad feeling—they just didn't know how to pinpoint the problems or come up with solutions. There are indicators you are probably already using, which we will cover first and then touch on other aspects that will provide you with more depth into the tech team without getting into the nitty-gritty. Being able to spot a divergence in any of the measures will help you find the likely culprit for the problem and be able to get help, either internally or by relying on external expertise, faster.

The Simple Stuff

If you have a sense that something is off about your tech team, that's probably because they are lacking in one of the obvious measures of health, which are delivery and quality. Both are very visible and do not require close inspection to tell when something is just not right.

Delivery is, put simply, getting things out of the door. Coders like to say that they "ship" code or features or "deploy to production." If said shipping is not happening as often as it should, you can decisively say something is not working. For example, feature deadlines tend to slip away if the team is not predictable. Estimates turn into "guesstimates," then mere guesses, and eventually mean nothing. I know that this is an issue for a company when I hear the other executives ignore estimates from R&D because they have learned those never mean anything.

Other than predictability, delivery also requires transparency. It is not rare for teams to realize that a certain task is more complex than they had initially thought and thus requires more time to complete. However, it can make all the difference in the world whether they communicate these discrepancies and help mitigate them immediately or only say that things will take longer when the deadline has whooshed by, and someone asks them for an update.

The complementing measure for delivery is quality, which can be described as "how well the things that got delivered perform." You might know that Meta (née Facebook) used to have a motto of "move fast and break things." The first part, moving fast, is about delivery. Breaking things meant that they were fine with a certain quality bar that was not too high, which as a concept I agree with (see the discussion about embracing failures in Chapter 7). However, it doesn't matter how fast you move when quality is allowed to spiral out of control. When Mark Zuckerberg realized that, he changed the company's motto to "move fast with stable infrastructure."

Quality can be measured externally by considering how many bugs are introduced with every new version release, the number of support requests the company receives, the rate of service outages, and how long it takes to recover from them (also known as "uptime"). When one of these spikes or diverges from industry standards, you can tell there is an issue.

Profitable Growth

Another indicator of a product engineering organization's health is how well it is scaling as the product becomes more complex and the company's business increases. For example, it is entirely reasonable that as the company becomes more successful and its market share grows, the product will require more expenses for servers or cloud costs and more personnel for maintaining these systems. However, the availability of venture capital in recent years meant that too many startups and companies that were scaling did not pay enough attention to how fast these costs were growing.

When you do not compare the team's growth with the value created, costs and headcount can precipitously spiral out of control. That is why we see public companies that, to "tighten their belts," laid off hundreds or even thousands of engineers without expecting to impact their offerings materially. They realized the problem too late and had let the organization grow too large and create a profligate culture.

For example, R&D headcount should not need to scale linearly with the company's growth merely to keep the lights on. Software is profitable precisely because, when executed properly, it can deliver new value to customers at a marginal cost that approaches zero. To help you picture how that is possible, consider a public company that wanted to achieve healthy growth when it came to developing its mobile applications. The product teams in charge of it spent the time to create a solution that streamlined the creation of the most straightforward screens and features. One engineer reported the result as a major new offering requiring minimal work on the applications themselves to implement. Thus, the engineers created a force multiplier rather than letting the system become more complex with time. In Figure 11.1, you can see the vast difference between profitable growth and the alternative.

Engineering Impact

At the end of the day, the purpose of a tech team is not to produce code but the business results that code is aimed to achieve. That is why you

Growth

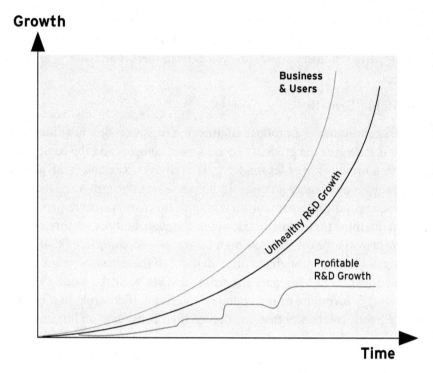

FIGURE 11.1
Profitable vs. unhealthy R&D growth.

should not merely measure a team by whether it has delivered everything it committed to do. I know I need to dig deeper when I see R&D groups that report 100% completion quarter after quarter. It often hides the fact that the plans are not ambitious enough. The team might prioritize low-hanging fruit instead of looking for opportunities with less certainty but considerably larger benefits. That is why the plethora of companies offering solutions for measuring the productivity of engineers or teams is not helpful at the executive level. While these tools can shed light on a problematic area in the team for the middle managers involved, merely tracking keyboard typing is not a good enough indicator at the macro level. These are what one would expect when managing a cost center and trying to keep costs to a minimum.

Impact means something different at every company, and even at yours, that definition has to evolve along with the rest of the business. Therefore it is not as straightforward to track as the previous indicators covered above, but that does not mean it is any less significant. Every company should come up with the metrics that make the most sense for it.

One example is tracking the innovation that is going on. Innovation is often a critical part of unlocking profitable growth and quicker delivery. We discussed a few possibilities for keeping track of your team's innovation in Chapter 6. No matter which of those you decide to use, experience shows that by merely tracking this and making it visible, companies see improvements in innovation. There is nothing wrong with leveraging the Hawthorne effect[2] to your advantage.

There are other examples of companies that have created other metrics for assessing their engineering impact. Perhaps the most well-known is Amazon's metric of how many press releases were made due to a team's delivered work. That is different from keeping track of how much work was delivered and helps keep the focus on outcomes and not the output itself. Famously, Amazon managers would kick off projects having already written the press release. That is precisely what I picture when I talk about aligning engineers on customer impact and focusing efforts where it matters the most.

I have also seen companies that decided to keep track of the bottom-line impact specific features had. If you give your product teams business goals to achieve with metrics for assessing their success in achieving those goals, you get this effect bundled in. Making sure to use metrics that guide the team in the right direction makes both their and your jobs easier.

ACTION ITEMS

These measures will serve to help you determine how well you are doing on your journey to capitalize on technology. No matter where you are along that road, deciding on a few and keeping track of them will help you establish a baseline and track your progress.

- Discuss with your executives the different measures for their own roles. Define together what success looks like.
- Spot weaker areas in your tech leadership and put in place a plan to address them.

- Have the delivery and quality of your tech team displayed in a way that is easy for everyone to access.
- Decide which engineering impact measures make the most sense for you and use them to guide the team.
- If you spot any issues, get help based on the area the metrics highlight. Sooner is better than later.

NOTES

1. Peter Pan employees are employees that, like the lost boys, seem to never mature and become more senior. https://avivbenyosef.com/peter-pan-employees/.
2. Coined after a set of experiments that showed a temporary increase in performance when people knew they were being observed. See https://en.wikipedia.org/wiki/Hawthorne_effect.

Conclusion

Having realized the importance of technology for your company's strategy, articulating a plan to maximize its effect should not require a grand effort that your already busy executive team does not have. By covering the principles of moving tech from a cost-center mindset to an innovation center, you understand how great tech executives behave, how R&D can look in *your* company, the importance of innovation, and how to tackle common problems in accountability, predictability, and alignment. Like Neo rising from the chair in *Matrix* and proclaiming he now knows kung fu, you now possess all it takes to lead your team to capitalize on tech's promise (though you admittedly had to spend more time than Neo).

Rather than merely putting this book down and continuing to the next one on your pile, take a second to ensure that you have made actionable steps based on what you have learned. Each chapter ends with a list of suggested action items, some of which require just a few minutes. You can find a summary of all these action items, along with videos about implementing them and more free resources, at https://capitalizing.tech/resources.

Further, you can get help implementing all of these and converse with your peers in my global community for executives in tech, the Leading Edge Club. You don't have to go it alone and can join at https://leadingedge.club.

I would love to hear your success stories or help fine-tune your approach if needed. Feel free to reach out to me at aviv@avivbenyosef.com.

Index

Page numbers followed by "n" refer to notes.